# WHY I WAS IMPRESSED TO WRITE A COOK BOOK.

It must appeal to the judgment of every thinking man and woman that the human family are more in need of sound, wholesome advice as to what they should eat and drink than ever before. The number of physicians and dentists increases each year at an alarming rate, but the aches and ills of the suffering people do not lessen. Thousands of people find themselves in a deplorable condition, with stomachs almost worn out, having depended largely upon predigested foods and a long list of so-called "dyspepsia cures."

The amount of patent medicines, "sure cures," consumed by the people in the United States is enormous, and is increasing every year. It must be apparent to all students of the past century that the people of the present are not enjoying the same degree of health as our ancestors, nor have we any assurance that things will improve unless some radical change is made.

Disease among cattle, poultry, and fish has increased so alarmingly in the last few years that we should no longer depend on the animal kingdom for food. We should look to the grains, nuts, vegetables, and fruits for a better dietary than can be prepared from the flesh of animals likely to be contaminated with tuberculosis, cancer, and other diseases.

In writing this book, the author has treated the subject from the commonly accepted definition of the term vegetarianism, which means to abstain from flesh food, but allows the use of eggs, milk, and its products. After years of experience in conducting vegetarian restaurants in several cities and making a study of the food question, he thinks he can bestow no greater gift upon the people than to place before them a book containing instruction in the preparation of wholesome dishes that will build up in place of tearing down the body.

In this work I do not claim to have reached perfection, nor to have exhausted the category of wholesome preparations and combinations within the domain of vegetarianism. In our efforts to teach how to live without the use of flesh foods, we find we have only begun to discover the inexhaustible resources of the great vegetable kingdom in the boundless wealth of varied hygienic foods.

E. G. F.

# HYGIENE OF COOKING

## GOOD COOKING

Good cooking is not the result of accident, a species of good luck, as it were. There is reason in every process; a law governing every chemical change. A course of medical lectures does not make a physician, nor will a collection of choice recipes make a cook. There must be a knowledge of compounding, as well as of compiling; of baking, as well as of mixing; and above all, one must engage in the real doing. Theory alone will not suffice; but experience, which practice only can give, is of the utmost importance.

Mention will be made under this head of those forms of cooking only which enter into vegetarian cooking as usually understood.

## BOILING

The term "boiling," as applied to cookery, means cooking in a boiling liquid. Many kinds of food need the action of water or other liquid, combined with heat, to cook them in the best manner, and boiling is one of the most common forms of cookery. When water becomes too hot to bear the hand in it with comfort, it has reached one hundred and fifty degrees, or the scalding point. When there is a gentle tremor or undulation on the surface, one hundred and eighty degrees, or the simmering point, is reached.

When there is quite a commotion on the surface of the water, and the bubbles breaking above it throw off steam or watery vapor, two hundred and twelve degrees, or the boiling point, is reached. After water reaches the boiling point it becomes no hotter, no matter how violently it may boil. The excess of heat escapes in the steam. This important fact is rarely understood by the average cook, and much fuel is often needlessly wasted because of the mistaken idea that rapidly boiling water cooks food more quickly.

In all ordinary cooking, simmering is more effective than violent boiling. The temperature of the water may be slightly raised by covering the kettle. If sugar or salt or anything to increase its density, is added to water, it takes longer for it to boil, but its boiling temperature is higher. This explains why boiling sugar syrup and boiling salt water are hotter than boiling fresh water. Boiling effects partial destruction or removal of organic and mineral impurities found in water, hence the importance of boiling the water where such impurities exist. Boiling also expels all the air and the gases which give fresh water its sparkle and vitality. Therefore, the sooner water is used after it begins to boil, the more satisfactory will be the cooking.

Fresh water should be used when the object is to extract the flavor, or soluble parts, as in soups and broths. Salt water should be used when it is desired to retain the flavor and soluble parts, as in most green vegetables. Cold water draws out the starch of vegetables. Boiling water bursts starch grains, and is absorbed by the swelling starch, and softens the cellulose in cereals and vegetables.

## MILK

In cooking some kinds of food, milk is used instead of water. Milk being thicker than water, less of the steam escapes, and it becomes hot sooner than water, adheres to the pan, and burns easily. At its boiling temperature (214 degrees), the casein contained in milk is slightly hardened, and its fat rendered more difficult of digestion. By heating milk in a double boiler, these dangers are avoided. It then only reaches a temperature of 196 degrees, and is called scalded milk. The process is a form of steaming.

## STEAMING

Steaming is a process of cooking food over boiling water. It is a very satisfactory and convenient method, without much loss of substance. It takes a longer time than some other ways of cooking, but requires less attention. There are two methods of cooking by steam: (1) In a steamer, which is a covered pan, with perforated bottom. This is placed over boiling water, and the steam carries the heat directly to the food. (2) By means of a double boiler. By this method the heat is conveyed from the boiling water, through the inner boiler to the food. When cooking by steam, the water should boil steadily until the food is done. Watery vegetables are made drier by steaming, and flour mixtures develop a different flavor than when baked.

## STEWING

Stewing is cooking in a small quantity of water at a low temperature for a long time, and is a form of boiling. The food loses less nutriment when stewed than when rapidly boiled.

## BAKING

Baking is cooking by means of dry heat, as in a close oven. The closely-confined heat of the oven develops flavors which are entirely different from those obtained by other forms of cooking. The baking of many kinds of food is as important as the mixing, and every cook should thoroughly understand how to regulate the oven. Nearly all flour mixtures, as bread, cakes, and many kinds of pudding, are more wholesome when baked than when cooked in any other way.

## BRAIZING

Braizing is a combination of stewing and baking. Meat cooked in a closely-covered stew-pan, so that it retains its own flavor and those of the vegetables and flavorings put with it, is braized. Braized dishes are highly esteemed.

## BROILING

Broiling, meaning "to burn," is cooking directly over, or in front of, the clear fire, and is the hottest form of cooking. The intense heat, combined with the free action of the air, produces a fine flavor quite unlike that obtained in any other way. Pan broiling is broiling on a hot surface instead of over hot coals.

# *SALADS*

## SALADS

All green vegetables that are eaten raw and dressed with acid, salt, and oil, are included in the list of salads, and they should always be served crisp and cool. Wash salad greens carefully, allowing them to stand in cold or iced water until crisp. Drain and wipe dry with a soft towel, taking care not to bruise the leaves, and keep in cool place till serving time. If they are not thoroughly dried, the water will collect in the bottom of the dish and ruin any dressing used.

Pare cucumbers thickly, and remove a thick slice from each end; cut into thin slices, or into one-half inch dice, and keep in cold water until ready to serve, then drain thoroughly; crisp celery in cold water also.

Pare tomatoes, and keep in a cold place, and sprinkle with chopped ice at serving time. The list of vegetables suitable for salads is so long that the question of kind is wholly a matter of choice. Asparagus, peas, string beans, beets, cauliflower, etc., are all well utilized in salads. Freshly cooked vegetables or left-overs may be used, but all cooked vegetables must be cold and perfectly tender. By deftly combining these left-overs with the favorite dressing, there is material for a delicious and economical salad, to which the somewhat aristocratic name of macedoine salad may be given. This salad may consist of a few or many kinds of vegetables, any combination pleasing alike to the eye and the palate being permissible, and if care is taken in the arrangement, it may be made a very attractive dish.

To the dressing of salads one must give utmost care and attention, as upon their excellence the success of the dish principally depends. While rules for dressings are innumerable, there are, after all, only a few really good ones. The French dressing and the mayonnaise are most generally known, the former being the simplest and most commonly used of all dressings. And it is quite the favorite for lettuce, cresses, chicory, and other vegetable salads. As the salad wilts if allowed to stand in the dressing, it should not be added till just at the moment of serving, and it is for this reason that it is frequently made at the table.

One of the most difficult things to prepare is a perfect mayonnaise, but once the knack is acquired, failure afterwards is rare. One essential point is to have all the materials cold. Chill in the refrigerator both the bowl and oil an hour or more before using. In warm weather it is advisable during the mixing to stand the bowl in a larger one of cracked ice. This dressing, if covered closely, will keep several days or longer in the ice-box. Keep in a cold place till wanted, as it liquefies as soon as mixed with meat or vegetables. To tone down the taste of the oil, and thus make more delicate salads, one may add to the dressing, just before it is used, a little cream beaten stiff and dry. This dressing is used with nut and fruit salads, and may be used with potatoes, tomatoes, celery, and other vegetables.

Most cooked vegetables intended for salads are moistened with a French dressing and allowed to stand an hour or more, or until well seasoned, in a cold place. To this process the term marinate is applied. Just before serving, pour off all the marinate that is not absorbed, and combine with the mayonnaise. A mistake frequently made in preparing salad dressing is that of using too much acid. The acid flavor should not predominate, but other flavors should also have their value.

## VEGETARIAN CHICKEN SALAD

Chopped protose, ½ pound.
Chopped celery, ⅔ cup.
Grated onion, 1 small teaspoonful.

Chopped nuttolene, ¼ pound.
Lemons, juice of 2.
Salt.
Mayonnaise, 2 tablespoonfuls.

Mix all together, adding mayonnaise dressing last. Serve on lettuce.

## ALMOND SALAD

Olives, 18.
Celery, 1½ cups.
Blanched almonds, 1½ cups.
Salad dressing.
Lettuce.

Stone and chop the olives. Add the almonds chopped, also the celery cut fine. Mix with salad dressing and serve on lettuce.

## NORMANDIE SALAD

Walnut meats, 1 cup.
French peas, 1 can.
Mayonnaise.
Lettuce.

Place walnut meats in scalding water about fifteen minutes, then remove the skins, and cut into pieces about size of a pea. Scald the French peas, and set aside for a while. Drain the water off the peas, and let them get cold; then mix with the walnuts. Pour mayonnaise dressing over all, and mix thoroughly. Serve on lettuce.

## BRAZILIAN SALAD

Ripe strawberries, 1½ cups.
Fresh pineapple, cut in small cubes, 1½ cups.
Brazil nuts, blanched and thinly sliced, 12.
Lemon juice, 4 tablespoonfuls.

Lettuce.
Dressing, 1 spoonful.

Cut the strawberries and pineapples into small cubes, and add thinly-sliced Brazil nuts that have been marinated in lemon juice. Arrange lettuce in rose-shape, and fill the crown with the above mixture, and cover with a spoonful of mayonnaise or golden salad dressing.

## NESSLERODE SALAD

Red cherries, ½ cup.
Black cherries, ½ cup.
Red currants, ½ cup.
White currants, ½ cup.
Sugar, 1½ cups.
Red raspberries, ½ cup.
Black raspberries, ½ cup.
Strawberries, ½ cup.
Lemon juice, ½ cup.

Pit the cherries, keeping them as whole as possible. Put a layer of fruit in the salad bowl, then a layer of sugar, then another layer of fruit, and so on, till all the fruit is used, finishing with a layer of sugar. Pour over all one-half cup of lemon juice. Shake the bowl gently from side to side, to draw out the juice until it nearly covers the fruit.

More sugar may be used if needed. This salad should be made two hours before using, and kept on ice.

## FRUIT SALAD

Apples, cut in half-inch cubes, 1 cup.
Bananas, cut in half-inch cubes, 1 cup.
Oranges, cut in half-inch cubes, 1 cup.

Mix all together and serve with golden salad dressing.

## WALDORF SALAD

Apples, cut in dice, 1½ cups.
Lemon juice, ½ cup.
Lettuce.
Celery, cut in dice, 1½ cups.
Mayonnaise dressing.

Mix apples, celery, and lemon juice well together, and pour mayonnaise dressing over. Serve on lettuce.

In making Waldorf salad use only crisp, white, tart apples, and the tender, white heart of the celery. The celery should be cut a little smaller than the apples. Use only white mayonnaise.

Drain off the lemon juice before adding the dressing, or it will ruin the mayonnaise.

## PROTOSE SALAD

Protose, cut in small dice, 1 pound.
Cold, boiled potatoes, cut into dice, 2.
Finely cut celery, ½ cup.
Finely minced onion, 1 tablespoonful.
Salt.
Celery salt, ½ teaspoonful.

Mix thoroughly with mayonnaise, and serve on lettuce leaves.

## PROTOSE AND CELERY SALAD

Diced protose, 2½ cups.
Grated onion, 1 tablespoonful.
Oil salad dressing.
Salt, 1 teaspoonful.
Crisp celery, 1¼ cups.
Lettuce or celery leaves.

Cut protose into half-inch dice, add a little salt, grated onion, and celery cut into the same size as protose. Set in ice-box, and just before serving pour over some of the oil salad dressing, and mix all together lightly. Serve on lettuce leaves or garnish with celery leaves.

## PEA AND ONION SALAD

Peas, canned or stewed, 4 cups drained.
Grated onion, 2 tablespoonfuls.
Lettuce leaves.
Mayonnaise.

Let peas drain half an hour, then add the onion. Mix well. Set in a cold place, and when ready to serve pour over the mayonnaise. Mix all together lightly, and serve on lettuce leaves.

## ENGLISH SALAD

Chopped lettuce, 1 cup.
Chopped celery, 1 cup.
Mayonnaise, 1 tablespoonful.
Lemons, juice of 2.

Mix lettuce, celery, and lemon juice thoroughly, then add mayonnaise and salt to taste.

## WATER LILY SALAD

Lettuce leaves.
Mayonnaise dressing
Eggs, hard-boiled, 8.

Cut crisp lettuce leaves into pointed strips, like the outer leaves of a water lily. Cut the whites of hard-boiled eggs also into strips, to make the petals. Mash all but two or three of the yolks, mix them with the mayonnaise, and fill in the center of the white petals. Take the remaining yolks and put through a fine sieve, and scatter this over the yellow center and white petals to resemble pollen of the flower.

## NUT AND FRUIT SALAD

Diced pineapple (canned), 1 cup.
Chopped walnuts, 1½ cups.
Diced oranges, 1 cup.
Diced dates, 1 cup.

Mix all together, and add golden salad dressing one hour before serving.

## NUT SALAD

Apple, 1 small.
Lettuce, ½ cup.
Onion juice, 1 teaspoonful.
Oil of cloves, 7 drops.
Salt.
Almonds, ½ cup.
Brazil nuts, ½ cup.
Sugar, 1 teaspoonful.
Lemon, juice of 1.

Chop all the ingredients moderately fine, and mix well with plenty of mayonnaise dressing.

## TOMATO MAYONNAISE

Tomatoes, 2.
Oil, ½ cup.
Onion juice, 3 or 4 drops.
Hard-boiled eggs, 2.
Raw egg, 1.

Peel the tomatoes, cut them in halves, and press out all the seeds, retaining only the solid, fleshy portion. Chop this fine; press through a sieve and drain.

Mash very fine the hard-boiled yolks of the eggs, and add the raw yolk. When thoroughly mixed, add the oil, a few drops at a time. When thick and smooth, add the dry pulp of the tomato, a little at a time. Stir in the onion juice. Serve on sliced protose or nuttolene.

## LIMA BEAN SALAD

Lima beans, 2 cups.
Strained tomatoes, 1¾ cups.
Hard-boiled yolks, 2.
Lettuce.
Nut butter, 2 tablespoonfuls.
Minced parsley, 1 tablespoonful.
Salt.
Sliced tomatoes.

Cook beans till well done, strain off the water, and set aside to cool. Mix nut butter as for table use, and thin it down with the tomato juice. Add the minced parsley and a little salt; turn this mixture on the beans, and stir well without breaking the beans. Mince the yolks of the hard-boiled eggs and sprinkle over the salad. Garnish with lettuce and sliced tomatoes, and serve.

## PEA AND TOMATO SALAD

Tomatoes, 6.
Nuttolene, 1 cup.
Salad dressing.
Green peas, 2 cups.
Lettuce.

Peel the tomatoes and scoop out the inside. Fill up with green peas and bits of nuttolene. Place each tomato on a lettuce leaf, and cover with salad dressing.

## LETTUCE

Separate the leaves and carefully wash to remove every particle of grit. Shake the water off the leaves. Place on a plate or in a salad dish, and send to the table for each to prepare as preferred.

Dress with lemon, salt, or olive oil. A mayonnaise or lettuce dressing may be provided for the table. If preferred, lettuce may be cut fine before being sent to the table.

## CABBAGE SALAD

Cabbage chopped very fine, 1½ cups.
Chopped walnuts, ½ cup.
Cream, ½ cup.
Lemon, juice of 1.
Sugar, 1 tablespoonful.
Salt.

Beat cream, sugar, and lemon juice together; then pour over the walnuts, cabbage, and salt, which have been thoroughly mixed.

## SALAD LA BLANCHE

Lima beans, 1 cup.
Minced celery, 1 cup.
Hard-boiled eggs, 2.
Minced lettuce, 1 cup.
Nuttolene, ¼ pound.

Boil the beans till tender, drain, and cool. Chop them rather fine, and add the minced celery, minced lettuce, nuttolene cut into small dice, and hard-boiled eggs finely chopped. Serve with La Blanche dressing.

## BEET SALAD

Cold, boiled beets.
Hard-boiled eggs.
Salt, olive oil, lemon juice.

Lettuce.

Arrange alternately slices of cold, boiled beet with slices of hard-boiled eggs on a plate. Season with salt, olive oil, and lemon juice poured over. Serve on lettuce.

## CARROT AND BEET SALAD

Carrots, 2.
Lettuce.
Dressing.
Beets, 2.
Celery.

Arrange alternately slices of cold, boiled carrots and beets. Serve on a lettuce leaf, garnish with finely-chopped celery.

Dress with olive oil, lemon juice, or French salad dressing.

## STUFFED BEET SALAD

Boil the beets whole till tender, selecting those of uniform size. Cut a slice off the bottom, so that they will stand upright, and scoop the inside out carefully. Take pains not only to avoid breaking the shell, but to keep the inside as nearly whole as possible. Peel the shells, and let them get perfectly cold. Cut the centers into tiny cubes, using an equal amount of parboiled potatoes and white celery cut to same size; mix well with mayonnaise or French dressing, and fill the shells, laying a slice of hard-boiled egg on top of each, and serving on a bed of tender lettuce leaves.

## TURNIP AND BEET SALAD

Turnips, 1¼ cups.
Green peas, 2 cups.
Mayonnaise.
Beets, 1¼ cups.

Lettuce.

Cook both vegetables separately till tender; dice and set on ice, until ready to serve. Place a spoonful of the mixed vegetables on a leaf of lettuce, border with green peas, and put a spoonful of mayonnaise on top.

## ASPARAGUS AND PROTOSE SALAD

Asparagus, 1½ cups.
Protose, 1½ cups.
Salt.
Mayonnaise.

Wash the asparagus and cut into pieces half an inch long. Boil in salted water till tender. Drain off the water, and when cold put into salad dish with protose cut into dice. Season with salt. Serve on a lettuce leaf with mayonnaise.

## BEET AND POTATO SALAD

Cut with a vegetable cutter or slice cooked beets and potatoes; arrange on a dish alternately, dress with cream salad dressing.

## BEET AND POTATO SALAD NO. 2

Beets, 1 cup.
Protose, ½ cup.
Onion juice, 2 tablespoonfuls.
Hard-boiled egg sliced, 1.
Mayonnaise.
Potatoes, 1 cup.
Egg yolks, ½ cup.
Salt.
Chopped parsley, ¼ cup.
Lettuce.

Cut the beets, potatoes, and protose into small dice. Mix all together and serve on a lettuce leaf; one slice of egg to each portion.

## ASPARAGUS AND CAULIFLOWER SALAD

Asparagus tips, boiled and drained, 2 cups.
Cauliflower, boiled, drained, cut in small pieces, 2 cups.

Dress with cream salad dressing.

## ASPARAGUS SALAD

Cut cooked asparagus tips into three-inch lengths, and serve on lettuce leaf with cream dressing.

## BRUSSELS SPROUTS SALAD

Put plain boiled Brussels sprouts into the ice-chest to get cold. Dress with olive oil and lemon juice. Serve on lettuce.

## DATE AND CELERY SALAD

Chop dates and celery, and serve with golden salad dressing.

## MACEDOINE SALAD

This is a mixture of any kind of cooked vegetables. Cover with French salad dressing, and serve on lettuce leaves.

# SALAD DRESSINGS

## MAYONNAISE DRESSING

Egg yolk, 1.
Cooking or olive oil.
Lemon juice.
Salt.
Sugar, 1 tablespoonful.

Into a saucer break the yolk of a fresh egg; add to it a large pinch of salt, and with a fork stir the yolk till it begins to stiffen. Gradually add to the yolk, a drop at a time, cooking oil or olive oil, stirring well after each drop is added. Continue this process till the mixture becomes too stiff to stir, then thin it with lemon juice, and add more salt. The salt helps to stiffen it. Thicken again with oil in the same manner as before, and thin again with lemon juice. Continue this till the desired amount is made. When stiff enough to cut with a knife, add one tablespoonful of sugar.

This will keep for a number of days, if set on ice. Success in making this depends upon the care with which the oil is added; at first, a drop at a time, and towards the last adding two or three drops, and perhaps half a teaspoonful at a time.

Note.—To make it keep well, add one tablespoonful boiling water, beaten in quickly. To keep from curdling, put lemon juice and oil on ice for fifteen minutes before using.

## WHITE DRESSING

    Egg yolk, 1, light colored.
    Salt.
    Cracked ice.
    Cream, whipped to stiff froth, 6 tablespoonfuls.
    Oil, 6 tablespoonfuls.
    Lemon juice, 1 tablespoonful.

Drop the yolk into a cold bowl, mix lightly, add a small pinch of salt; then add the oil drop by drop. The dressing should be very thick. Stand the bowl in another containing a little cracked ice, so that you may be constantly reducing the color of the egg. Now add slowly the lemon juice, then stir in the whipped cream. This dressing, if properly made, should be almost as white as whipped cream, while having the flavor of mayonnaise. Serve with Waldorf salad.

## BOILED SALAD DRESSING

    Eggs, 5.
    Melted butter, ¼ cup.
    Lemon juice, 4 tablespoonfuls.
    Salt, 1 level teaspoonful.
    Sugar, 1 level teaspoonful.
    Rich cream, 1 cup.

To the yolks add the salt and sugar; beat with an egg whisk until thick and light, then add gradually the melted butter and lemon juice. Cook over hot water until the mixture thickens and falls away from the sides of the pan. Take from stove, put into a glass jar, and when cool cover closely. When ready to use pour into it lightly the rich cream whipped to a stiff, dry froth. If whipped cream can not conveniently be obtained, plain sweet or sour cream may be used in the dressing, but it will not be so light and flaky.

## CREAM SALAD DRESSING (PLAIN)

Lemon juice, ½ cup.
Sugar, 1 tablespoonful.
Rich milk or cream, ½ cup.
Olive oil, 1 tablespoonful.
Salt, 1 teaspoonful.
Eggs well beaten, 2.

Put the lemon juice into a granite dish on the stove, and add the olive oil, sugar, and salt. Put the milk or cream on the stove in another saucepan, and when hot add the beaten eggs. Let cook smooth, but do not allow it to boil or it will curdle. Remove from the stove, and when partially cool beat the two sauces together. This is a very nice dressing for vegetable salads.

## CREAM SALAD DRESSING

Cream, 1 cup.
Milk, cold.
Butter, size of walnut.
Salt, 1 level teaspoonful.
Lemon juice, 4 tablespoonfuls.
Corn starch, 1 rounded teaspoonful.
Eggs, 2.
Sugar, 1 level teaspoonful.

Put the cream into a double boiler; when scalding hot add the corn starch dissolved in a little cold milk, and cook about five minutes, stirring constantly. Then add the butter. To the yolks of the eggs add the salt and sugar; beat till light and thick, then add alternately the lemon juice and the hot cooked mixture. Fold in the stiffly beaten whites, and set aside to become cold.

This dressing may be used the same as mayonnaise.

## WHITE CREAM SALAD DRESSING

Make same as cream salad dressing, omitting the yolks of the eggs.

## FRENCH SALAD DRESSING

Oil, 3 tablespoonfuls.
Salt.
Lemon juice, 1 tablespoonful.
Onion juice, ¼ teaspoonful.

Mix and pour over the salad.

## LETTUCE DRESSING

Hard-boiled eggs, 3.
Lemon juice, ½ cup.
Lettuce.
Olive oil, 1 tablespoonful.
Salt.

Mash the yolks smooth and fine, add the olive oil and salt. Mix well, and add gradually the lemon juice. Beat thoroughly, then pour the dressing over the lettuce. Cut the whites of the eggs into rings and lay on top. Serve as soon as dressed.

## GOLDEN SALAD DRESSING

Pineapple juice, ¼ cup.
Lemon juice, ¼ cup.
Beaten eggs, 2.
Sugar, ⅓ cup.

After beating the eggs well, add the pineapple juice, lemon juice, sugar, and small pinch of salt. Beat together and cook in double boiler. Let boil about two minutes.

## NUT OR OLIVE OIL SALAD DRESSING

Olive oil, ½ cup.
Water, ¼ cup.

Lemon juice, ¼ cup.
Salt, 1 teaspoonful.
Beaten eggs, 3.

Beat all well together in the dish; set dish in hot water over the fire, and stir constantly till thickened. As soon as it begins to thicken remove from the fire and place in a dish of cold water, stirring until it cools, and set on ice till cold. It is then ready for use.

## OIL SALAD DRESSING (SOUR)

Lemon juice, 2 teaspoonfuls.
Olive oil, ¼ cup.
Salt, ½ teaspoonful.
Water, 2 teaspoonfuls.
Eggs, 2.

Heat together in double boiler, stirring constantly. When it begins to thicken, place into cold water and stir until cold.

## GREEN MAYONNAISE

Make as ordinary mayonnaise. Use two light-colored yolks and six tablespoonfuls of oil. Chop enough parsley to make one tablespoonful; put it into a bowl, and with a knife rub it to a pulp. Then add gradually to the mayonnaise. Add a teaspoonful of the lemon juice. Use for fruit salad, white grapes, and pulp of shaddock. Mix, and serve on lettuce leaves.

## DRESSING LA BLANCHE

Butter, 1½ dessertspoonfuls.
Flour, 1 heaped dessertspoonful.
Salt.
Egg, 1.
Lemon juice, ¼ cup.

Melt the butter in a frying-pan, but be careful not to brown it. When hot, stir in the flour, well-beaten yolk, lemon juice, and salt to taste. Stir this dressing through the vegetables, and serve on a garnish of crisp lettuce.

# *SOUPS*

## SOUPS

Cream soups are seasonable at any time, using any vegetable in its season. Canned goods may be used when the fresh article is not obtainable.

Vegetables that are too tough and old to cook in any other way may be used in soups to advantage. If it can be afforded, a teaspoonful of whipped cream may be dropped into each plate, and will be found very delicious.

By a puree is meant a thick soup; it differs but little from cream soup, being perhaps a trifle thicker. If properly made, cream soups and purees are dainty, delicious, and nourishing.

Fruit soups are in favor during hot weather, for dinners and luncheons; they are very easily made, and are wholesome and refreshing. Any desired fruit juice may be thickened with corn starch, sago, or arrowroot, and served with or without fruit.

Fruit soup should always be served cold, in glass sherbet cups, with a layer of chipped ice on top.

## KINDS OF SOUP

Observing these proportions and following the foregoing directions, delicious cream soups are made of rice, squash, celery, peas, asparagus, cucumber, spinach, peanuts, potato, corn, lima beans, cauliflower, beets, tomato, salsify, chestnut, mushrooms, onions, baked beans, lentils, macaroni, spaghetti, watercress, string beans, sago, tapioca, barley, carrots, etc. All vegetables should be cooked very tender in boiling salted water, drained, and rubbed through a sieve. Rice, sago, tapioca, and barley should be boiled slowly till each grain is soft and distinct. Roasted peanuts are chopped fine; chestnuts are boiled and mashed; macaroni and spaghetti are cut into very small pieces, after boiling till tender. String beans are to be minced before adding to the soup.

## CREAM SOUPS, FOUNDATION OF

Rub one heaping tablespoonful of butter and two of sifted flour to a cream; melt in a saucepan over the fire, and add slowly four cups milk, stirring constantly. When it thickens add salt and whatever seasoning and ingredient is desired to make the soup.

## CROUTONS FOR SOUP

Take thin slices of bread, cut them into little squares, place them in a baking pan, and brown to a golden color in a quick oven.

## EGG BALLS FOR SOUP

Egg yolks, hard boiled, 6.
Salt, 1 teaspoonful.
Flour, ½ tablespoonful.
Egg yolks, raw, 2.

Rub the hard-boiled yolks and flour smooth, then add the raw yolks and the salt. Mix all well together, make into balls, and drop into the soup a few minutes before serving.

## EGG DUMPLINGS FOR SOUP

Milk, 1 cup.
Flour.
Eggs, 2.

Beat the eggs well, add the milk and as much flour as will make a smooth, rather thick batter, free from lumps. Drop this batter, a tablespoonful at a time, into the boiling soup.

## NOODLES FOR SOUP

Beat one egg till light, add a pinch of salt and flour enough to make a stiff dough. Roll out very thin; sprinkle with flour to keep from sticking. Then roll up into a scroll, begin at the end, and slice into strips as thin as straws. After all are cut, mix them lightly together, and to prevent their sticking together keep them floured a little till you are ready to drop them into the soup, which should be done a few minutes before serving. If boiled too long they go to pieces.

## VEGETABLE BOUILLON

Vegetable soup stock, 2 quarts.
Cooked and strained tomatoes, 2 cups.
Bay leaves, 2.
Salt, 1 tablespoonful.
Onions, grated, medium size, 2.

Mix all the ingredients together, and let simmer slowly two or three hours. There should be about one quart of soup when done; strain, reheat, and serve.

## NUT CHOWDER SOUP

Nuttolene or protose, ¼ pound.
Hard-boiled eggs, 3.

Browned onions, 3.
Sage, 1 teaspoonful.
Thyme, 1 teaspoonful.
Bay leaves, 2.
Salt, 1 tablespoonful.

Chop all together till fine, then add to strained boiling tomatoes, four cups; add boiling water, one cup; thicken with flour, one tablespoonful; reheat and serve.

## NUT FRENCH SOUP

Vegetable soup stock, 1½ quarts.
Tomatoes, cooked, strained, 2 cups.
Sage, ¼ teaspoonful.
Browned flour, 1 tablespoonful rounded.
Onions, large, 1.
Bay leaves, 2.
Thyme, ½ teaspoonful.
Salt to taste.

Slice the onion and mix all the ingredients together, excepting the salt; boil slowly one hour; strain, reheat, salt, and serve. This soup requires plenty of salt to bring out the flavor.

## MOCK CHICKEN SOUP

Butter, ¼ cup.
Onion, medium size, 1.
Celery stalks, 1.
Milk, 1¼ quarts.
One egg.
Flour, 2 tablespoonfuls.
Parsley, chopped fine, 1 teaspoonful.
Nuttolene, 3 tablespoonfuls.
Flour.

Put butter in saucepan with the onion, parsley, and celery; cook it to a golden brown color; add the flour and cook until brown, being careful not to scorch. Now add the milk boiling hot and stir briskly to prevent lumping. Add the nuttolene. Beat the egg with enough flour to make a stiff batter, but thin enough to pour; pour this into the boiling stock, stirring at the same time. This will appear as small dumplings in the soup. Let simmer twenty or thirty minutes; salt, and serve.

## MOCK CHICKEN BROTH

    Small white beans, 2 cups.
    Small onion, 1.
    Salt.
    Hot water, 8 cups.
    Celery salt.
    Butter.

Wash, then stew the beans in hot water with the onion for three hours, stewing down to six cups; strain, and add a pinch of celery salt and a small piece of butter. Salt to taste. This broth may be served to the sick instead of beef tea.

## PLAIN VEGETABLE SOUP (1)

For soup stock.

    Water, 6 cups.
    Strained tomatoes, 2 cups.

Shave in fine shreds, add to soup stock, and cook moderately for two hours.

    Carrot, 1.
    Potato, 1.
    Leek, 1.
    Turnip, 1.
    Onions, 2.
    Celery stalk, 1.

Add a little sage and thyme. When done, run through puree sieve or colander, and add a little chopped parsley and salt to taste.

## PLAIN VEGETABLE SOUP (2)

Butter, 2 tablespoonfuls.
Flour, 1 tablespoonful.
Chopped onion, 1.
Chopped carrots, ½ cup.
Chopped potatoes, ½ cup.
Chopped turnips, ½ cup.
Chopped celery, ½ cup.

Place in heated saucepan, stir often to prevent burning, add a little more butter if necessary; brown till vegetables are quite soft, then add

Strained tomatoes, 2 cups.
Hot water to proper consistency.

Season with parsley and salt to taste. Simmer till done.

## WHITE SOUBISE SOUP

Bread, 4 or 5 slices.
Onions, 4.
Salt, 1 teaspoonful.
Butter, 1 teaspoonful.
Rich milk, 2 cups.
Potatoes, 2.
Flour, 1 teaspoonful.
Water, 4 cups.

Soak the bread in the milk, boil onions and potatoes in water until well done, and mix with the bread and milk; add salt and flour rubbed in the butter; strain all through a fine sieve; bring again to the boiling point, but do not allow it to boil; serve. If too thick, add a little boiling water.

## JULIENNE SOUP

Fresh peas, ⅓ cup.
Chopped potatoes, ¾ cup.
Tomato, ¼ cup.
Soup stock, 1 quart.
Carrots cut in dice, ½ cup.
Chopped turnips, ⅓ cup.
Minced onion, 1.
Chopped parsley.

Cook the turnips and carrots together in just enough water to prevent scorching, the potatoes and onions in the same manner, the peas by themselves. When all are done, mix together and add the soup stock, salt, and parsley; reheat, and serve. The water the vegetables are cooked in should be used in the soup.

## TOMATO SOUP

Soup stock, 3 cups.
Nut butter, 1 tablespoonful.
Strained tomatoes, 2 cups.
Salt.

Add tomatoes to soup stock, also the nut butter mixed smooth and thin in a little of the tomato; heat to boiling, salt, and serve.

## BEAN AND TOMATO SOUP

Boiled beans, 1 cup.
Butter, 1 tablespoonful.
Cooked rice, ¼ cup.
Salt.
Stewed tomatoes, 1 cup.
Flour, 1 tablespoonful.
Boiling water to required consistency.

Rub beans and tomatoes through a sieve; add salt and butter rubbed in flour; then add cooked rice and enough boiling water to make the proper consistency; reheat, and serve.

## TOMATO-VERMICELLI SOUP

Strained tomatoes, 3 cups.
Vermicelli, ½ cup.
Water, 2 cups.

Cook the vermicelli in the tomato till done and add water; if too thin, bind with a little thickening of butter and flour. A rounded tablespoonful of each will be enough for each quart of soup.

## TOMATO AND OKRA SOUP

Onion, large, 1.
Butter.
Stewed tomatoes, 2 cups.
Soup stock or water, 4 cups.
Thinly sliced okra pods, 2 cups.
Flour, 1 teaspoonful.
Nut butter, 1 teaspoonful.
Chopped parsley.
Salt.

Brown onion in a saucepan with a little butter; add flour, nut butter, tomatoes, parsley, and okra. Add the soup stock or water and cook slowly for three hours. Season with salt, and serve.

## WHITE SWISS SOUP

Rice, ½ cup.
Onion, small, 1.
Rich milk, 1½ cups.
Flour, ½ teaspoonful.
Water, 2 cups.

Potato, 1.
Egg yolk, 1.
Salt.

Boil the rice in the water, and add the onion and potato. When the vegetables are well done add the rich milk and bring to a boil. Beat well the yolk of the egg with the flour and stir in the boiling soup. Let it boil, season with salt, rub through a sieve; reheat, and serve.

## CORN AND TOMATO SOUP

Kornlet, ground fine, 1½ cups.
Strained tomatoes, 2 cups.
Water, 1 cup.

Mix thoroughly, season with salt, heat to a boiling point, and serve.

## CEREAL CONSOMME

Cooking oil, ¼ cup.
Chopped onion, 1.
Flour, 1 tablespoonful.
Crushed protose, ½ pound.
Caramel-cereal, 1 cup.
Salt.
Barley, ¼ cup.
Carrot, small, 1, finely chopped.
Boiling water, 6 cups.
Bay leaf.

Place in the soup kettle the cooking oil and barley; brown barley till quite brown; add onion, carrot, flour, and brown the vegetables till quite tender; add the protose and boiling water; let simmer very gently for six hours, adding boiling water from time to time. Keep the original amount. Stir often to prevent burning. Half an hour before the soup is done add the caramel-cereal, bay leaf, and salt; press through a fine colander, and simmer to six cups.

## SWISS LENTIL SOUP

Lentils, 1 cup.
Small onion, 1.
Browned flour, 2 rounded tablespoonfuls.
Salt.

Put lentils to cook in a large quantity of boiling water; boil rapidly a short time, then simmer without stirring. When they begin to get tender and are yet quite moist, slice an onion and press into the lentils until covered; keep the vessel over a slow, even fire, until the lentils are well dried out. The drying-out may be finished in the oven if the lentils are covered so that they will not harden on top. When well dried add a little boiling water and rub through a fine colander, removing the hulls. Into this pulp stir the browned flour. Beat till smooth, then add gradually enough boiling water to make of consistency of soup; salt, boil, and set where it will keep hot twenty minutes to an hour, to blend ingredients.

## SPRING VEGETABLE SOUP

Green peas, 1 cup.
Onion, 1.
Egg yolk, 1.
Soup stock, 3 cups.
Salt.
Shredded lettuce, 1 head.
Parsley, 1 small bunch.
Water, 1 cup.
Butter, size of egg.

Put in the stew-pan the lettuce, onion, parsley, and butter, with the water; let simmer till tender; season with salt; when done strain off the vegetables and put two-thirds of the liquid in the stock. Beat up the yolk with the other third. Put it over the fire, and at the moment of serving add this with the vegetables to the soup.

## TURNIP AND RICE SOUP

Turnip, medium sized, 1.
Milk, 3 cups.
Butter.
Washed rice, ⅓ cup.
Cream, 1 cup.
Croutons or toast.

Pare a medium-sized turnip, slice, and put with rice and butter into saucepan with sufficient water to cook; let simmer till tender, rub through a fine sieve and return to the saucepan. Mix in enough milk to make of the proper consistency; stir over the fire and let simmer ten or fifteen minutes; then stir in a lump of butter and cream; serve with croutons.

## GERMAN LENTIL SOUP

Lentils, ¾ cup.
Carrot, a few slices.
Nut butter, 1 tablespoonful.
Celery, one sprig, or a little celery salt.
Salt.
Water, 4 cups.
Turnips, a few slices.
Apple sauce, ½ cup.
Onion, 1.

Boil lentils in the water with the onion, carrot, turnip, and celery; boil gently about one and one-half hours; put through a sieve and return to soup kettle; add nut butter and apple sauce. Bring to a boil, salt, and serve.

If necessary, add a little boiling water or rich milk to thin the soup.

## LENTIL AND TOMATO SOUP

Lentils, 1 cup.
Water, 4 cups.
Nut butter, 1 tablespoonful.

## RICE SOUP

Rice, ¼ cup.
Salt, 1 teaspoonful.
Milk, 3 cups.
Butter, 1 tablespoonful.
Water, 3 cups.
Egg yolk, 1.
Flour, 2 teaspoonfuls.

Boil the rice in the water for forty minutes, or until perfectly soft, adding salt; add sufficient boiling water from time to time to keep the original amount; press through a sieve and thicken with well-beaten yolk of egg, milk, flour, and butter. Add a little more salt if necessary; serve with toasted crackers or zwieback sprinkled with crumbs of cottage cheese.

## LIMA BEAN SOUP

Lima bean soup may be prepared same as white bean soup, omitting the tapioca.

## BREAD BISQUE

Dry sifted bread crumbs, one cup, added to cream soup, four cups.

## TOMATO BISQUE NO. 1

Tomatoes, ½ quart can.
Flour, 1 tablespoonful.
Nut butter, 1 tablespoonful.
Milk, 4 cups.
Butter, 1 tablespoonful.
Salt.
Bay leaf, 1.
Onion, small, 1.

Place butter in pot, add one bay leaf, one small onion; let braize till light brown, add flour, and stir until flour is well mixed; add hot milk, slowly stirring constantly to keep smooth; add nut butter, which should be emulsified first with the tomato, then add slowly stirring briskly; salt, heat thoroughly, strain; reheat, serve.

## TOMATO BISQUE NO. 2

Strained tomatoes, 4 cups.
Peanut butter, about 4 tablespoonfuls.
Salt.

Put tomatoes in double boiler, set on the range, and when scalding hot add the nut butter emulsified in enough water to pour readily, mix together and salt to taste. Use plenty of salt to bring out the flavor.

## ROLLED OATS SOUP

Chopped onion, 1.
Celery salt.
Left-over porridge, 1 cup.
Milk, 2 cups.
Butter, 1 tablespoonful.
Bay leaf.
Water, 2 cups.
Salt, 1 teaspoonful.

Into a saucepan put the chopped onion and butter; cook carefully, without browning the butter, until the onion is perfectly soft; then add celery salt, bay leaf, and porridge; stir for a moment, then add water and milk; bring to a boil and strain; add salt, reheat, and serve.

## FAMILY FAVORITE

Soup stock, 4 cups.
Sliced okra, 1 pod.

Salt.
Stewed tomatoes, ½ cup.
Water, 1 cup.

Mix all together and boil one hour; strain, reheat, and serve.

## NUT MEAT BROTH

Water, 4 cups.
Almond meal, 1 cup.
Gluten meal or browned flour, 2 tablespoonfuls.
Salt.

Let all boil together thoroughly, and serve.

## PEA SOUP WITH VEGETABLE STOCK

Scotch peas, 1 cup.
Vegetable soup stock, 4 cups.
Mint, ¼ teaspoonful.
Salt.

Cook peas till soft and put through a fine colander to remove the hulls. Add soup stock and mint, reheat, salt, and serve.

A cup of cream is a great improvement to this soup.

## SAVORY POTATO SOUP

Vegetable soup stock, 4 cups.
Potatoes, medium size, 2 or 3.
Mint, ⅓ teaspoonful.
Chopped onion, 1.
Salt, 1 teaspoonful.
Marjoram, ¼ teaspoonful.

Cook the potatoes and onion till soft. Put through a colander, add the soup stock, mint, marjoram, and salt, which have been simmered together half an hour. Heat well, and serve.

## CELERY AND TOMATO SOUP

Celery heart, 1.
Soup stock, 2 cups.
Celery salt.
Tomato, 2 cups.
Salt.

Chop celery rather fine, and cook in a little water till tender; add the tomato, salt, and soup stock; heat well, and serve.

## NUT AND CREAM OF CORN SOUP

Sweet corn rubbed fine, 1 quart can.
Vegetable soup stock, 4 cups.
Salt, 1 heaping tablespoonful.

Bring to a boil, rub through a colander, reheat, and serve.

## ARTICHOKE SOUP

Artichokes, 6.
Onions, small, 2.
Sage, ¼ teaspoonful.
Lemon juice, 1 tablespoonful.
Salt.
Water, 2 quarts.
Protose, ⅛ pound.
Bay leaf.
Browned flour, 1 tablespoonful.

Select prime, green, globe artichokes before they have developed; cut off the stems, trim off the hard leaves round the bottom, and cut off the upper quarter of the artichoke leaves. Put the water in soup kettle; add the artichoke, onions, and protose. Let simmer gently for two hours, then add sage, bay leaf, and lemon juice. Thicken with browned flour. Let all boil together a few minutes, then press through a colander, salt, reheat, and serve.

## IMPROMPTU SOUP NO. 1

Onion, 1.

Slice into heated saucepan with

Savory or green herbs, 1 pinch.
Butter, 1 tablespoonful.

Let brown two or three minutes, then add

Nut butter, 1 tablespoonful.

Brown a little longer, then add

Stewed tomatoes, 1 cup.
Hot water, 3 cups.

Let all boil together and thicken with gluten; salt, strain, and serve.

## IMPROMPTU SOUP NO. 2

Malted nuts, ½ cup.
Browned flour, 1 tablespoonful.
Flour, 1 tablespoonful.

Mix, and dissolve in a little milk, then add

Milk, 3 cups

and heat to boiling point, stirring often to prevent scorching; set back far enough to keep from boiling, then whip into the broth

Eggs well beaten, 4.

Salt, and serve.

## CREOLE SOUP

Water, 2 cups.
Tomatoes, 1 pint.
Clove of garlic, 1.
Small turnip, 1.
Boiled rice, heaped tablespoonful.
Small carrot, 1.

Boil all together, season with a little salt, rub the vegetables through a sieve, and thin to the consistency of cream with hot water or nut cream.

## PALESTINE SOUP

Jerusalem artichokes, 12.
Celery, 1 sprig.
Boiled cream, 1 pint.
Croutons.
Leek, 1 sprig.
Salt.
Nutmeg.

Wash and peel the artichokes, put over them cold water sufficient to cover, add leeks, celery, and salt. Simmer an hour and a half. Press through a sieve, put back on the stove, and beat into it a pint of boiled cream. Add a little nutmeg. Serve with croutons. If too thick, add a little hot milk or cream.

## FRUIT SOUP (PINEAPPLE)

Thicken pineapple juice with arrowroot. Serve cold with a bit of pineapple glace in each cup.

## CHOCOLATE SOUP

Chocolate (Sanitas), ¼ pound.
Water, 2½ cups.
Sugar, 2 tablespoonfuls.
Flour, 1 tablespoonful.
Milk, 1 quart.
Ground cinnamon, 1 teaspoonful.
Whipped cream, 1 cup.

Soak the chocolate in two cups of the water; when soft put to cook; when it boils add the sugar and flour rubbed smooth in the rest of the water. Cook slowly for five minutes and add the hot milk. Strain, stir in the cinnamon and whipped cream. Serve at once with crisps or wafers. Blanched almonds toasted are served with the soup.

## FRUIT SOUP

Strawberry, or other juice, 1 cup.
Pineapple juice, 1 cup.
Lemon juice, 1 tablespoonful.
Sago, 1 tablespoonful.
Sugar, 1 tablespoonful.
Chipped ice.

With the strawberry or other juice cook the sago; add the pineapple juice and sugar; cool, and serve in sherbet cups with chipped ice.

## FRUIT SOUP (SWEDISH)

Boil prunes and raisins slowly till tender, sweeten and save the juice; boil sago till clear, mix with the fruit and juice, and serve very cold.

## FRUIT SOUP (ORANGE)

Thicken orange juice with arrowroot, and serve very cold in cups with a bit of candied orange peel on top of each glass.

### FRUIT SOUP (LEMON)

Make a strong lemonade, thicken with arrowroot, serve very cold with a bit of candied lemon peel or candied ginger in each glass.

### FRUIT SOUP (MARQUISE)

Take two parts red raspberry juice and one of currant, sweeten, thicken with arrowroot and sago; candied orange peel or blanched and shredded almonds are a dainty addition.

### FRUIT SOUP (CRANBERRY)

Thicken some sweetened cranberry juice with arrowroot, and serve cold in cups, as a first course at a Christmas or New Year's dinner.

### FRUIT SOUP (GRAPE)

Thicken bottled grape juice with arrowroot, and serve cold with chipped ice. This is refreshing for invalids.

### FRUIT SOUP (CHERRY)

Thicken cherry juice with arrowroot, and serve with other fruit soups; garnish with black cherries in their season.

### FRUIT SOUP (STRAWBERRY)

Thicken fresh strawberry juice with arrowroot and put on ice to chill; put a layer of chipped ice on top of each cup before serving, and lay a ripe strawberry, stem and all, on top of each glass.

## RAISIN, APPLE, OR PRUNE SOUP

Either seedless raisins, apples, or prunes may be added to sago soup. The soup should then bear the name of the fruit used.

# ENTREES

## MOCK WHITE FISH

Rice flour, ⅓ cup.
Butter, 1 scant teaspoonful.
Mace, ¼ teaspoonful.
Salt to taste.
Milk, 1 cup.
Onion grated, 1 tablespoonful.
Potatoes, mashed, 3 cups.

Heat the milk to boiling, stir in the rice, flour, butter, onion, mace, and salt. Cook all ten minutes, stirring frequently. Have the potatoes ready, freshly cooked and mashed; while hot add the rice mixture, and put into a pan to cool. When cool, cut in slices about five inches long, dip in egg and crumbs, put in oiled pan, and bake until nicely browned. Serve with parsley sauce.

## FILLETS OF VEGETARIAN SALMON

Milk. 1½ cups.
Farina, ½ cup.
Tomatoes, cooked and strained, ½ cup.
Egg, 1.

Salt to taste
Nuttolene, ½ cup.
Eggplant, boiled and mashed, 1½ cups.
Bread crumbs, fine and dry, 1 cup.
Color, vegetable red enough to make salmon color.

Cook and mash the eggplant, stir the nuttolene to a cream in a little of the milk, then add the rest of the milk, the eggplant, tomatoes, and salt. Set in double boiler; when scalding hot, add the farina and bread crumbs. Mix thoroughly and let cook fifteen or twenty minutes. Remove from the range, stir in the raw egg and the color, mixing till the color is perfectly blended. Turn into a deep pan to cool; should be about two inches deep. When cold cut into slices, egg, crumb, and bake. Serve with parsley sauce.

## PROTOSE ROAST WITH OLIVE SAUCE

Protose, ¾ pound.
Chopped onion, small, 1.
Parsley, 1 tablespoonful.
Boiling water, 2 cups.
Butter, 1 tablespoonful.
Bread crumbs, 2 cups.
Eggs, 2.
Salt to taste.

Put the onion, parsley, and butter into the boiling water, and thicken with bread crumbs stiff enough to cut nicely when done. Into this mixture put one hard-boiled egg chopped fine, and break in one raw egg to make it hold together. Salt to taste. Put a layer of this filling into a baking-pan, then a layer of protose cut in thin slices, then a layer of the filling, and another layer of the protose, and last another layer of the filling. Bake in a moderate oven one hour. Serve with olive sauce.

## MOCK TURKEY WITH DRESSING

German lentils, 1 cup.
Chopped walnut meats, ½ cup.

Milk, 1 cup.
Salt.
Celery salt.
Granola or bread crumbs.
Minced onion, ¼ cup.
Chopped celery, 1 cup.
Eggs, 2.
Sage.
Sliced bread.

1. Thoroughly wash the lentils and soak overnight. Boil slowly until tender and run through colander. Add the walnut meats, one egg, and the minced onion browned with the chopped celery in a little oil. Add salt and sage to taste. Thicken with granola or bread crumbs.

2. Dip thin slices of bread in a mixture of one egg and a cup of milk, or thin slices of nuttolene may be used instead.

Make alternate layers of 1 and 2.

## DRESSING NO. 1

Stale bread crumbs.
Hot milk, 2 cups.
Eggs, 1 or 2.
Butter, 1 tablespoonful.

Mix bread crumbs with hot milk, eggs, and butter. Season with salt, sage, and onions. Serve with cranberry sauce.

## DRESSING NO. 2

Large onions, 2.
Fresh bread crumbs, 1 cup.
Milk, ¾ cup.
Sage, 1 tablespoonful.
Beaten eggs, 2.
Chopped parsley, 2 tablespoonfuls.
Butter, ¼ cup.

Salt to taste.

Peel onions and parboil. Drain and chop fine. Soak bread crumbs in the milk; then mix all ingredients together. Stir the mixture over the fire until it is reduced to a thick paste, without allowing it to boil.

Serve a slice of the roast with a spoonful of dressing on one end and cranberry sauce on the other.

## ROAST DUCK (VEGETARIAN STYLE)

Lentil pulp, 1¾ cups.
Minced onion, ¼ cup.
Chopped parsley, ⅓ cup.
Stale bread crumbs, ground fine, 1 cup.
Eggs (one hard-boiled), 3.
Butter, 1 teaspoonful.
Chopped walnuts, ½ cup.

Take lentil pulp, one hard-boiled egg chopped fine, one beaten egg, minced onion, and chopped parsley browned in a little oil, one teaspoonful of butter, and salt to taste. Mix well and put one-half of this mixture in an oiled baking pan, then a layer of the following mixture: Stale bread crumbs soaked in hot water, chopped walnuts, a little grated onion, one egg, and salt and sage to taste. Finish with a layer of the lentil mixture. Bake, and serve with gravy.

## NUTTOLENE ROAST

Nuttolene, 1 pound.
Bread crumbs.
Hot water, 1 quart.
Salt and sage to taste.

Put the nuttolene through a vegetable press, or work smooth with a knife or spoon; add the hot water and beat to a cream. Add salt and sage, and thicken with bread crumbs stiff enough to retain its shape when moulded.

Press into a deep buttered bread-pan and bake till nicely browned. Turn out of the pan and slice. Serve with any good brown sauce or walnut gravy.

## MOCK VEAL LOAF

Nuttolene, ¼ pound.
Minced protose, ½ pound.
Egg, well beaten, 1.
Milk, ¼ cup.
Sage, ¼ teaspoonful.
Ground mace, ¼ teaspoonful.
Butter size of an egg.
1 small onion, braized in the butter.

Cracker or zwieback crumbs enough to make a stiff mixture. Mix all together, salt to taste, and bake in a deep bread-pan. Garnish with parsley or young celery hearts.

## VEGETARIAN ROAST

Nut food, ⅓ pound.
Onion, ½.
Egg, 1.
Hot water, 2 cups.
Butter, 2 teaspoonfuls.
Bread crumbs or granola.

To the water add the nut food minced, minced and browned onion, and butter. Thicken with toasted bread crumbs or granola until quite stiff. Add the beaten egg, salt, and a little sage if desired. Put in oiled pan and bake. Serve with gravy.

## ROAST OF PROTOSE

Protose, 1 pound.
Strained tomato, ½ cup.
Chopped onion, 1.

Nut butter, 2 tablespoonfuls.
Browned flour, 2 tablespoonfuls.
Sage.

Cut the protose lengthwise through the center, then cut each half in six pieces. Place in a deep baking-pan, let the first piece lean slantingly against the end or side of the pan, the second against the first, and so on. Sprinkle this with finely chopped onion, and a little powdered sage, and pour over it a nut cream made of two heaping tablespoonfuls of nut butter emulsified, in enough hot water to cover the protose. Add to this the browned flour, rubbed smooth in a little tomato. Salt to taste. A little celery salt may be used if desired. Cover and bake till the gravy is thick and brown.

## HAMBURGER LOAF

Lentils, raw, 1 cup.
Protose, ½ pound.
Cooking oil, 2 tablespoonfuls.
Salt.
Chopped onion, ½ cup.
Eggs, 5.
Bread crumbs.

Cook the lentils until tender, then simmer as dry as possible. Put through a colander, brown the onions in oil, and add to the lentils, together with the protose and two of the raw eggs. Mix salt to taste, and add enough bread crumbs so that it will mold nicely.

Have the three remaining eggs boiled hard and the shells removed. Put one-half the loaf mixture into a bread-pan, then put the three hard-boiled eggs in a row through the center and cover with the remaining mixture. Press down gently and bake. Serve with sauce imperial.

## NUT AND GRANOLA ROAST

Minced nut food, ¼ pound.
Onion, 1.
Oil, 1 tablespoonful.

Egg, 1.
Boiling water, 2 cups.
Granola.

Brown the onion in the oil, then add the minced nut foods and boiling water. Thicken with granola. Stir in the raw egg, and a little sage or thyme if desired. Salt to taste. Put in oiled pan and bake. Serve with gravy.

## CREAM NUT LOAF

Dried bread crumbs, 2 cups.
Ground sweet corn, 1 cup.
Ground Brazil nuts, 1 cup.
Eggs, 2.
Sage.
Mashed peas, 1 cup.
Mashed potatoes, 1 cup.
Cream, ½ cup.
Salt.

Mix all thoroughly together, press in a deep bread-pan, and bake a nice brown. Serve with a sauce made of one part sweet cider and two parts grape juice, thickened with a little corn starch.

## IMPERIAL NUT ROAST

Pea pulp, 1½ cups.
Chopped walnuts, 1½ cups.
Bread crumbs, 1 cup.
Sage.
Lentil pulp, 1½ cups.
Egg, 1.
Salt.
Milk to moisten.

Mix the peas, lentils, and walnuts with salt to taste. Put a layer in a deep bread-pan, then put a layer made of the crumbs, eggs, milk, sage, and salt.

This should be just stiff enough to spread easily. Cover with the remaining pea and lentil mixture. Baste with cream, put in the oven, and brown.

## WALNUT LOAF

Chopped walnut meats, ½ cup.
Egg, 1.
Boiling water, 2 cups.
Olive oil or butter, ½ tablespoonful.
Bread crumbs, 2 cups.
Salt to taste.

Mix walnut meats and crumbs together, pour over the boiling water, mix well, add the raw egg, butter, and salt, stir thoroughly, press into buttered bread-pan, and bake.

## WALNUT ROAST

Granola, 2 cups.
Ground walnuts, 1 cup.
Milk or cream, 1 quart.
Eggs, 4.

Soak the granola in the milk or cream for ten minutes and add the walnuts, eggs, salt, and a dash of nutmeg. Mix the preparation well. Grease a baking-pan, turn in the mixture, and bake thirty-five to forty minutes.

## CEREAL ROAST

Cream, 4 Cups.
Nut meal, 1 cup.
Onion, chopped fine, 1.
Sage.
Gluten, ½ cup.
Bread crumbs, 1¼ cups.
Salt.

Mix all together and bake in a moderately hot oven.

## NUT AND TOMATO ROAST

Celery, 1 root.
Granola, 1½ cups.
Eggs, 5.
Nuttolene, ½ pound.
Tomatoes, 2 cups.
Onions, 3.
Protose, ½ pound.

Chop the celery and onions fine, put into a saucepan with enough cooking oil to prevent burning, and cook until a rich brown, stirring occasionally. Add to this one quart of boiling water and the tomatoes. Boil for fifteen to twenty minutes. Then remove and strain as much as possible through a soup strainer. Take three and one-half cups of this gravy and mix with it the granola, eggs, and salt to taste. Have ready the protose and nuttolene cut into thin slices. Put in a layer of the granola mixture into a big baking-pan, then a layer of protose, then granola, then nuttolene, and so on until all is used, finishing with the granola mixture. Bake forty-five minutes or until a nice brown. Remove from the fire, let cool a little, turn out on a platter, and serve with the remaining gravy.

## DRIED PEA CROQUETTES

Dried peas, 1½ cups.
Egg, 1.
Salt.
Olive oil, 2 teaspoonfuls.
Bread crumbs.

Cover the peas with water and soak overnight. Drain and cook in fresh boiling water until tender. Drain, press through a colander, add a little salt and olive oil. Mix thoroughly and form into small rolls about three inches long. Dip in beaten egg, roll in bread crumbs, and bake in a quick oven. Serve with tomato sauce.

## CHICKEN CROQUETTES

Mashed potato, ½ cup.
Toasted bread crumbs, ½ cup.
Nut butter, ¼ cup.
Hard-boiled egg, chopped fine, 1.
Browned onion, ¼ cup.
Sage, 1 teaspoonful.
Hot water, ½ cup.
Chopped walnuts, ¼ cup.
Minced nuttolene, 2 tablespoonfuls.
Beaten egg, 1.
Boiled rice, 1 cup.
Salt, 3 teaspoonfuls.

Mix all together and form into croquettes; dip into beaten eggs and milk, roll in browned bread crumbs which have been oiled or buttered, and bake.

## HASHED PROTOSE CROQUETTES

Protose, 1 pound.
Butter, 1 tablespoonful.
Salt.
Potatoes, 1 pound.
Eggs, 4.
Mace.

Boil the potatoes, mash, add the minced protose, the yolk of three eggs, salt, and mace. Mix thoroughly, form into oblong croquettes; egg, crumb, and bake.

## EGG MIXTURE FOR CROQUETTES, FILLETS, ETC.

Break an egg into a bowl or deep saucepan, break up with a fork, add a tablespoonful of hot water to soften the albumen of the egg, and mix till free from lumps, but do not beat in too much air. Dip the croquettes in the egg, roll in crumbs, and bake.

## PROTOSE WITH BROWNED POTATOES

Peel and slice potatoes three-fourths of an inch thick. Cut protose in strips same thickness. Place in a pan two slices of potatoes and one of protose, and repeat same until the pan is full. Pour over this vegetable stock sufficient to cover. Bake in the oven till the potatoes are done and nicely browned.

## NUT FRICASSEE WITH BROWNED SWEET POTATOES

Cut some nut food into half-inch cubes and pour over it a thick, brown or white gravy sufficient to cover well. Let it simmer about one hour. Peel and steam or boil potatoes until tender, but not overdone. Put them in a baking dish with a little butter or olive oil, salt, and bake in a quick oven until nicely browned. Serve with the fricassee.

## FRIJOLES WITH PROTOSE MEXICANO

Mexican beans, ½ cup.
Vegetable stock, 1 cup.
Mace.
Diced protose, ¼ pound.
Strained tomatoes, 1 cup.
Salt.

Cook the beans in just enough water to prevent scorching. When done, have ready a stock made of the vegetable stock, tomatoes, mace, and salt. Pour over the beans, together with the protose, and let simmer for an hour or more.

## FRICASSEE OF PROTOSE WITH POTATO

Serve a spoonful of nice white mashed potato on an empty platter; press a slice of broiled protose up against the potato, and serve with a spoonful of brown gravy. Garnish with parsley.

## GREEN CORN AND TOMATO

Corn pulp, 3 cups.
Strained tomatoes, 1 cup.
Butter, 1 tablespoonful.
Salt.

Scrape the given amount of corn from the cob, add the tomatoes and butter, simmer until the corn is tender; salt, and serve as a vegetable.

Cold boiled corn cut from the cob may be substituted for the fresh corn, if desired.

## MOCK CHICKEN RISSOLES

Protose, ½ pound.
Nuttolene, ½ pound.
Milk, ½ cup.
Mace.
Flour, 1 tablespoonful.
Butter, ¼ cup.
Salt.

Put the butter into a saucepan; when hot stir in the flour, and stir until brown; add the hot milk, salt, and mace, and let cook a few minutes. Chop the nut food fine and mix into the sauce. Have ready some tart shells made of rich pie paste; fill with the mixture. The sauce should be cool before adding the nut food.

## NEW ENGLAND BOILED DINNER

Potatoes, 4½ cups.
Turnips, 1 cup.
Onions, 2 cups.
Carrots, 1¾ cups.
Cabbage, 2½ cups.

Cut the potatoes, carrots, and turnips in three-quarter inch cubes; slice the onions and cut the cabbage into pieces about one and one-half inch square. Boil the potatoes and onions together. The carrots turnips and cabbage may also be cooked together in salted water. When all are done, mix together, and serve with slices of protose or other nut food that has been braized in a tomato or brown sauce.

## NUT AND VEGETABLE STEW

Nuttolene, 1 cup.
Turnips, ¾ cup.
Chopped celery, ½ cup.
Bay leaf, 1.
Salt.
Carrots, 1½ cups
Potatoes, 1½ cups.
Onion, small, 1.
Butter, 1 lump.

Put all on, except nuttolene and potatoes, and boil one hour. Then add potatoes and nuttolene and cook slowly until potatoes are done. Salt to taste. Thicken with a little flour, work smooth with a lump of butter. A little protose might also be added.

## STEWED PROTOSE (SPANISH)

Butter, 1 tablespoonful.
Minced parsley, 1 tablespoonful.
Tomatoes, 4 cups.
Onions, 4.
Flour, 2 tablespoonfuls.
Protose, 1 pound.

Put the butter into a saucepan and add the sliced onion, minced parsley, and cook ten minutes. Then stir in the flour, mix well, and add the tomatoes. Stir well to free from lumps. Cover and cook twenty to thirty minutes. Slice the protose into small pieces and simmer in sauce ten minutes. Salt, and serve.

## PROTOSE FRICASSEE

Tomatoes, 1 cup.
Minced parsley, 1 teaspoonful.
Protose, 1 pound.
Vegetable stock, 2 cups.
Mixed herbs, ½ teaspoonful.
Onion, 1.
Eggs (yolks), 2.

Mince the onion and braize in a little butter or olive oil five minutes; add the minced parsley strained tomatoes, mixed herbs, and vegetable broth. Bring to a boil and add the protose, cut into cubes or diamonds of one-half inch. Cook for a few minutes and thicken with a few spoonfuls of flour rubbed smooth in a little water. Salt to taste, and serve. Just before serving add the beaten yolks.

## PROTOSE STEAK SMOTHERED IN ONIONS

Protose, ¾ pound.
Cooking oil, ½ cup.
Salt.
Onions, large, 6.
Vegetable stock, 2 cups.

Cut the protose into twelve slices, lay half of them in an oiled baking-pan; have the onions sliced and lightly browned in the oil. Cook half of the onions over the protose, then put on the rest of the protose, then the remainder of the onions, pouring the vegetable stock over all. Salt to taste. Bake until the stock is reduced to a rich brown gravy.

## PROTOSE SMOTHERED WITH TOMATOES

Protose, ¾ pound.
Butter, ½ cup.
Salt.
Tomatoes, 12.
Sugar, 2 tablespoonfuls.
Celery salt.

Cut protose into twelve slices and cut each tomato in half. Put one slice of tomato in a baking-pan; on this put a slice of the protose, then a slice of tomato on top, and so on, making twelve orders in all. Chop the butter in little pieces and sprinkle over, also the salt and celery salt. Cover and bake until the tomato is nearly done. Then remove the cover and brown very lightly. Serve two slices to each person, garnished with parsley.

## PROTOSE POT ROAST

Protose, ¾ pound.
Strained tomatoes, 1 cup.
Vegetable soup stock, 2 cups.
Salt to taste.

Mix the vegetable stock with the strained tomatoes, salt to taste, and pour over the protose, which has been sliced and placed in a baking-pan. Bake one hour.

## BRAIZED PROTOSE AND CABBAGE

Braize protose according to the recipe, and serve with boiled cabbage.

## PROTOSE STEAK WITH POTATOES SMOTHERED IN ONIONS

By putting a layer of sliced raw potatoes in the bottom of the pan and covering with the protose, onions, and stock, we have protose steak and potatoes smothered with onions.

## PROTOSE PILAU

Water, ¾ pint.
Rice, cooked, 1 cup.
Butter, 1 teaspoonful.
Protose, ½ inch cubes, ¼ pound.
Minced onion, 1 tablespoonful.

Let simmer ten or fifteen minutes; thicken with browned flour, two heaping teaspoonfuls, mixed with strained tomatoes to consistency to pour easily. Salt and celery salt to taste.

## PROTOSE PATTIES (PLAIN)

Protose, 1 pound.
Salt.
Cream, 3 tablespoonfuls.
Eggs, 2.
Bread crumbs.

Thoroughly crush the protose and mix with the salt and one egg. Form into patties, roll in egg and cream, then in bread crumbs. Bake in greased pan till lightly browned. If desired, the crumbs may be slightly moistened with cream.

## BRAIZED PROTOSE

Protose, 12 slices.
Vegetable stock, No. 2, 3 cups.
Sage.
Minced onion, medium size, 1.
Butter.

Butter a deep pan and sprinkle with the minced onion and sage. On this lay the slices of protose, cut a little less than half an inch thick. Cover the pan and put into the oven to brown, turning the protose once, and watching carefully that the onions do not burn. Remove from the oven and cover with the vegetable stock. Cover and return to the oven, and bake until the stock is reduced to a thick, brown gravy.

### PROTOSE CUTLETS WITH MASHED POTATO

Protose, ½ pound.
Milk, 1 cup.
Brown sauce.
Egg, 1.
Granose flakes.

Cut protose into six slices as for protose steak. Dip in beaten egg and milk, and roll in granose flakes. Do this the second time, and bake in brown sauce about thirty minutes. Serve with mashed potato.

### NUT LISBON STEAK

Protose, 6 large slices.
Brown gravy, 3 cups.

Broil or fry the protose a nice brown (but do not burn) and drop into the gravy (any good brown gravy will do); let simmer an hour or two. Serve hot with a spoonful of the gravy.

More protose may be used if desired.

### PROTOSE AND TOMATO

Protose, 6 large slices.
Tomato, cooked and strained, 2 cups.
Corn starch, 1 teaspoonful.
Salt to taste.

Cut the protose in rather thick slices and lay in a flat baking-pan (one about two inches deep will answer nicely); boil the tomatoes and thicken with the corn starch; add the salt, and pour over the protose. Bake slowly in a moderate oven. Do not bake too dry. The protose should be nice and juicy with the tomatoes when done. The corn starch may be omitted if desired.

## BAKED PROTOSE WITH MACARONI

Macaroni (not cooked), 1½ cups.
Oil, 1 tablespoonful.
Flour, ⅓ cup.
Salt.
Minced protose, 1 cup.
Minced onion, medium size, 1.
Milk, 2 cups.

Break the protose in one-inch lengths. Drop in three quarts of boiling water, previously salted. Boil from one-half to three-quarters hour, turn into colander, and pour cold water over it. Drain and turn into baking-pan.

## SAUCE

Put the oil in a stew-pan, add the onion, braize till nicely browned, then add the flour, and stir until brown. Add the milk, then the protose. Season with salt. Pour this sauce over the macaroni and sprinkle with bread crumbs. Bake in a moderate oven till brown.

## FRIZZLED PROTOSE IN EGGS

Protose, 1 pound.
Eggs, 8.
Olive oil.

Cut the protose into small, thin, narrow strips; put into a frying-pan with a little olive oil, and when hot pour the well-beaten eggs over it, stirring constantly, until the eggs are set. Serve hot on toast.

## ESCALLOPED PROTOSE

Protose, 1 pound.
Bread crumbs, ¾ cup.
Potatoes, medium size, 4.
Brown sauce, sufficient to cover.

Slice one-half the potatoes in a baking dish, sprinkle one-half the bread crumbs over them; on the crumbs put half the protose cut into thin slices; pour over some of the gravy to moisten. Add the remainder of the ingredients in the same manner, making two layers. There should be sufficient gravy to cover and cook the potatoes and protose.

## EGGPLANT BAKED WITH PROTOSE

Eggplant, medium size, 2.
Chopped onion, large, 1.
Salt.
Protose, ¾ pound.
Vegetable stock.

Peel and slice the eggplant in one-fourth inch slices, and cut the protose into twelve slices. Put a layer of the eggplant in an oiled pan, then a layer of protose, and sprinkle part of the onion over all. Make another layer with the remainder and cover with vegetable stock. Salt to taste, cover, and bake. Tomato may be used in place of the stock if desired.

## PROTOSE JAMBALAYA

Butter, 1 tablespoonful.
Minced onion, 1.
Minced garlic, small, 1.
Flour, 1 tablespoonful.
Tomatoes, 1½ cups.
Vegetable stock, 1½ quarts.
Rice, 1 cup.
Minced protose, ¾ pound.
Minced celery, ¼ cup.
Salt, mace, and bay leaves.

Put the butter into a saucepan, heat, add the onion and garlic, and brown, then add the flour and brown, add the tomato, and cook a few minutes, stirring to prevent flour from lumping. When nice and brown, add vegetable stock and the seasoning; boil until the ingredients are well blended; add the rice and boil till the rice is tender, stirring often. To this add the minced protose that has been heated in a covered dish in the oven. Mix and serve.

## RAGOUT OF PROTOSE

Protose cut in irregular pieces, 1 pound.
Hot water, 4 cups.
Browned flour, 1 tablespoonful.
Celery salt.
Strained tomatoes, 1½ cups.
White flour, 1 tablespoonful.
Salt.

Put all together, except the flour, and let simmer thirty or forty minutes, adding enough boiling water from time to time to keep the original quantity. Thicken with the flour, and serve.

## PROTOSE CUTLETS

(1) Protose, minced, 1 pound.

Season with

Salt.
Lemon juice.
Sage.

Add a little

Chopped parsley.

Make a heavy white sauce with

(2) Flour, 2 tablespoonfuls.

Milk, ¾ cup.

If desired, flour may be rubbed with

Butter, 1 tablespoonful.

Add salt to taste.

Mix 1 thoroughly with 2. When cool, make into patties, cutlets, or croquettes. Dip into beaten egg, roll in bread crumbs that have been moistened with melted butter, and brown in the oven.

## PROTOSE CHARTREUSE

Vegetable stock, 2 cups.
Egg, 1.
Salt.
Protose, ½ pound.
Rice, cooked, 1 quart.
Bread crumbs, sufficient to thicken.

To the stock add the protose, bread crumbs, the egg unbeaten, and salt. Mix thoroughly. Line a baking-pan with part of the rice, and fill in the center with the protose mixture; cover with the rest of the rice, and press down gently. Bake, and serve with browned sauce.

## PROTOSE STEAK

Split a pound of protose in two lengthwise, and cut into as many slices as needed. Broil in a pan, and serve with brown sauce.

## PROTOSE STEAK A LA TARTARE

Minced protose, 1 pound.
Butter, 1 tablespoonful.
Mayonnaise, 3 tablespoonfuls.
Onion, 1.

Eggs, 6.
Onions and olives mixed, to garnish.

Put the butter in a saucepan and set on the range. When hot, add the onion and cook until brown; add the minced protose, a pinch of salt, and mix. Form into balls, making a depression in each ball, and drop an egg yolk in each depression. Bake until the eggs are done. Chop the onions and olives, add the mayonnaise, and use as a garnish.

## PROTOSE OR NUTTOLENE CUTLETS

Protose or nuttolene, 6 slices, each large enough for a cutlet.
Eggs, 3.
Cream or rich milk, 2 cups.
Bread crumbs, buttered, 1½ cups.
Salt.

Beat the eggs, add the milk and salt, dip the slices of nut food in this, and then in the buttered bread crumbs, and lay in a greased baking-pan. Place the remaining bread crumbs with the milk, add salt, and pour over the cutlets. If not enough to cover, a little milk may be added. Put into the oven and bake till the mixture sets, or it may be placed on the range, and when one side is browned turn and brown the other side.

## GOLDEN NUT CHARTREUSE

Vegetable stock, 2 cups.
Corn meal mush, 1 quart.
Bread crumbs.
Egg, 1.
Protose, or other nut food, ½ pound.
Salt.

Make the filling same as for protose chartreuse; line the pan with the mush, put in the filling, and cover with mush. Bake, and when cold cut into slices, egg, crumb, and bake. Serve with gravy.

## LENTIL HASH

Lentils, 1 cup.
Potatoes, medium size, 2.
Rice, 2 tablespoonfuls.
Egg, 1.
Onion, large, 1.
Tomato, 1.
Cooking oil, ¼ cup.
Garlic, small piece.

Boil the lentil, onion, tomato, potatoes, and rice together till soft; chop very fine and add the cooking oil, egg, and a very small piece of garlic, and salt to taste. Put into oiled pan and bake until brown.

## LENTIL FRITTERS

Lentils, 1 cup.
Rich milk, ¼ cup.
Egg, 1.
Butter, 1 tablespoonful.
Flour, ¾ cup.

Cook lentils until tender, drain, press through a colander, add the milk, butter, flour, salt, and beaten yolk. Mix thoroughly and add the stiffly-beaten white. Drop in spoonfuls on oiled griddle and brown on both sides, or bake in the oven. Garnish with parsley, and serve with marmalade or apple sauce.

## WALNUT LENTIL PATTIES

Cooked lentils, 2 cups.
Eggs, 2.
Chopped walnuts, ¾ cup.
Granola, or bread crumbs.

Rub the lentils through a colander and add the chopped walnut meats, one egg, and a pinch of salt. Thicken with bread crumbs or granola. Form into patties, roll in egg and buttered crumbs, and bake. Serve with gravy.

## LENTIL PATTIES ON MACARONI

Lentils, 1 cup.
Eggs, 2.
Chopped parsley, 1 teaspoonful.
Minced onion, 2 tablespoonfuls.
Olive oil, 2 tablespoonfuls.
Bread crumbs.

Cook the lentils until tender and put through a colander. To this pulp add the rest of the ingredients, using sufficient bread crumbs to make stiff enough to form into patties. Dip the patties in egg and crumbs. Brown in the oven. Serve on a platter with creamed macaroni.

## WALNUT LENTILS

Lentils, 1½ cups.
Walnuts, 1 cup.
Butter.

Cook the lentils in six cups of water until quite tender and the water almost dried away. Press the lentils through a soup strainer. Grind the walnut meats and add to the lentils. Add a little butter and salt to taste.

## LENTIL ROAST

Lentils, 1½ cups.
Butter, 1 tablespoonful.
Granola, 1 cup.
Eggs, 2.
Onion, small, 1.
Mixed herbs, 1 teaspoonful.
Ground walnuts, 1 cup.
Salt.

Cook the lentils in sufficient water to prevent burning. When tender, add the sliced onion, butter, mixed herbs, and salt to taste. Cook with the pot closely covered for twenty-five to thirty minutes longer.

Remove from fire, drain, press through a colander, and add the granola, ground walnuts, and eggs. Mix well, press into a baking pan, and bake forty-five minutes or until nicely browned.

## LENTIL NUT ROAST

Lentil pulp, 2 cups.
Egg, 1.
Toasted bread crumbs or granola.
Nut butter, ½ cup.
Dairy butter, 2 teaspoonfuls.

Emulsify the nut butter in enough water to mix easily. Mix all together and thicken with toasted bread crumbs or granola. Salt to taste. Put in oiled pan and bake. Serve with gravy. A little thyme or sage may be used if desired.

## RICE MOLD

Rice, 1 cup.
Milk, ⅔ cup.
Lemon or vanilla flavoring.
Egg, 1.
Sugar, 2 tablespoonfuls.
Stewed fruit.

Wash clean and boil the rice in two quarts of water until done. Drain off the water well. Add, while hot, a custard made of the egg, milk, and sugar. Flavor with lemon or vanilla. Form into molds, and serve with stewed prunes, peaches, or any other kind of fruit.

## RICE AND BANANA COMPOTE

Rice, ¾ cup.
Milk, 3 cups.
Vanilla.
Bananas, 6.
Sugar.

Bring the milk to a boil, thicken with corn starch or flour, and add sugar to taste. Simmer the bananas in this sauce for half an hour. Add vanilla.

Rice for bananas: Cook the rice in two and one-fourth cups of water in a double boiler till done. The rice should be soft and each grain standing out separate when done. Make a layer of the rice, and serve the bananas on it.

## RICE AND EGG SCRAMBLE

Rice, 2 cups.
Eggs, 4.
Milk, 4 cups.

Thoroughly wash the rice and boil in salted water until tender and drain. Scramble the eggs in the milk, add salt when nearly done, mix with the rice, and serve hot.

## SPANISH RICE

Rice, 1 cup.
Garlic, medium size, ½.
Bay leaf, 1.
Minced celery, 1 stalk.
Tomatoes, 2 cups.
Minced onion, small, 1.
Oil, 2 tablespoonfuls.
Mace, ½ teaspoonful.
Flour, 2 tablespoonfuls.
Salt.

Boil the rice until about half done, drain, and finish cooking in the following sauce:—

Put the oil in a saucepan, add all the other ingredients except the tomato and flour; set over the fire and stir occasionally, to prevent burning, until brown. Then add the flour and stir till brown. Add the tomato, let cook a few minutes, strain, and add to the rice.

## CORN FRITTERS

Green corn pulp, 1 pint.
Milk, 4 tablespoonfuls.
Flour, ½ cup.
Eggs, 4.

Mix the corn, milk, flour, and yolks of the eggs together thoroughly. Then fold in the well-beaten whites of the eggs, and fry by spoonfuls.

## PROTOSE AND RICE CHOWDER

Protose, ½ pound.
Rice, cooked, 1 cup.
Potatoes, ½ pound.
Butter, 1 tablespoonful.
Vegetable stock, 1 cup.
Bread, ¼ loaf.
Cream, or milk, 1 cup.
Salt and mace to taste.

Put the butter in a deep dish, melt, then add a layer of the protose, sliced quite thin, then sprinkle with mace, salt, and bits of butter. Then add a layer of the sliced potatoes, sprinkle with part of the rice, then a layer of bread, then more salt, bits of butter, and minced onion. Add the remainder in the same order, and pour over all one cup of hot vegetable stock. Cover, set on range, and let simmer one-half hour, then pour over all one cup of hot cream or milk, and serve.

## NOODLES

Butter, 1 tablespoonful.
Salt, ¼ teaspoonful.
Eggs, 2.
Flour, to make a very stiff dough.

Whip the egg until light, add the salt, and work in the flour, making a smooth, stiff dough. Roll out thin, in a long narrow strip, sprinkle with flour to prevent sticking, and roll up into a long roll, rolling crosswise. Then with a sharp knife cut into very thin slices and drop into boiling salted water. Cook about twenty minutes. Drain, pour over the melted butter, and serve hot.

## VEGETABLE OYSTER A L'ITALIENNE

Take macaroni broken into one-inch lengths, and boiled until tender, and vegetable oyster which has been parboiled twenty minutes, and put in alternate layers in a baking-pan. Pour over this a sauce made from both of the liquors (macaroni and vegetable oyster) thickened with the yolks of the eggs. Sprinkle with granola and bake until browned.

## GREEN CORN CHOWDER (NEW ENGLAND STYLE)

Corn pulp, fresh cut from the cob, 2½ cups.
Diced protose, 1 cup.
Vegetable stock, 1 cup.
Parsley, chopped, 1 tablespoonful.
Bread crumbs.
Minced onion, medium size, 1.
Sliced potatoes, 2 cups.
Oil, 2 tablespoonfuls.
Salt.

Brown the onion in the oil, and add the protose and vegetable stock. When thoroughly heated, add corn pulp, mix all together, heat up well, and salt. Put the sliced potatoes in cold water, drain, and put into a pan of flour; shake the pan so as to cover the potatoes with flour. Put half of the potatoes in a layer in the bottom of a baking-pan, cover with half the corn and protose mixture, sprinkle with bread crumbs and part of the parsley. In the same manner add the remainder of the potatoes and mixture. Moisten with stock and bake until the potatoes are done.

### SQUASH FRITTERS

Mashed summer squash, 2 cups.
Butter, 1 heaping tablespoonful.
Sugar, 1 tablespoonful.
Salt, ½ teaspoonful.
Rich milk, ½ cup.
Flour, 1 cup.
Eggs, 2.

Mix thoroughly the squash, butter, milk, flour, sugar, salt, and beaten yolks. Then fold in the stiffly-beaten whites. Brown on a griddle.

### BEAN CROQUETTES

Navy beans, 1 cup.
Olive oil, 1 tablespoonful.
Bread crumbs.
Salt, 1 level teaspoonful.
Beaten egg, 1.

Cover beans with water, soak overnight, drain, and cook in fresh boiling water until tender, or about an hour. Drain, press through a colander, add salt and olive oil. Mix thoroughly and roll into cylinder-shaped croquettes; dip into beaten egg, roll in bread crumbs and bake in moderate oven. Serve with tomato sauce.

### SCOTCH PEA LOAF

Scotch pea pulp, 1½ cups.

## MACARONI WITH TOMATO SAUCE

Macaroni, raw, 1 cup.
Flour, 1 tablespoonful.
Cream, ½ cup.
Tomatoes, stewed and strained, 2 cups.
Salt to taste.

Break the macaroni into one-inch lengths and boil in salted water till thoroughly done. Boil tomatoes and thicken with flour, rubbed smooth in a little water. Add the cream, which should be hot, and salt to taste. Drain the macaroni, pour the sauce over, mix well, and serve. The cream may be omitted if preferred.

## MACARONI CUTLETS

Macaroni, raw, 1 cup.
Flour, 2 heaping tablespoonfuls.
Minced protose, 1 cup.
Salt to taste.
Milk, 1 cup.
Egg, 1.
Bread crumbs.

Boil the macaroni in salted water till done, drain, and chop fine. Boil the milk and thicken with the flour; stir in the well-beaten egg; beat thoroughly. Add the macaroni, protose, and salt, and make stiff with the bread crumbs, so that it can be made into cutlets. Make into any shape desired. Put into an oiled pan and bake till nicely browned. Serve with tomato or cream sauce.

## CREAMED MACARONI

Rich milk, 2 cups.
Flour, 2 large tablespoonfuls.
Salt.
Macaroni, 1 cup.

Butter.

Boil the macaroni and put it into a gravy made of the milk, flour, butter, and salt. Mix well, and serve.

## MACARONI IN CREAM

Macaroni, 2½ cups.
Milk, 4 cups.
Egg yolk, 1.
Cream, 1 cup.

Cook the macaroni in plenty of boiling water thirty minutes. Turn off the water and wash the macaroni by pouring two or three quarts of cold water over it. Return the macaroni to the saucepan and add the boiling milk. Remove to a cool part of the stove and cook for thirty minutes. Before serving, add the beaten yolk and the boiling cream. Shake the pot to mix the egg with the macaroni. Stir as little as possible. Salt to taste.

## EGG MACARONI

Macaroni, 1½ cups.
Eggs, hard-boiled, 3.
Cream gravy, 2 cups.
Bread crumbs.

Break macaroni into one-inch lengths and boil in salted water till tender. Drain and wash with cold water. Put into a baking dish and sprinkle over it the hard-boiled eggs chopped fine. Stir into cream gravy, made from rich milk, sprinkle top with bread crumbs. Bake until nicely browned.

## BAKED MACARONI WITH EGG SAUCE

Macaroni, 2 cups.
Milk, 3 cups.
Granola.

Eggs, 4.
Salt, 1 tablespoonful.

Break the macaroni into inch lengths and boil in salted water thirty to thirty-five minutes. Drain, turn it into a deep pan. Pour over this a custard made with the milk, beaten eggs, and salt. Sprinkle with granola on top, and bake in a moderate oven thirty minutes.

## MACARONI WITH APPLE

Butter a deep baking-dish and put in a layer of mashed and sweetened apple sauce. Grate a little nutmeg over and add a layer of cooked macaroni. Repeat till the dish is full, finishing with the apple sauce. Bake till the apples are slightly browned. Serve with sweetened cream, seasoned with nutmeg. May be served as a dessert.

## MACARONI AND CHEESE (VEGETARIAN STYLE NO. 1)

Macaroni, 2½ cups.
Egg sauce, 1 cup.
Sour cream, ½ cup.
Granola.

Break the macaroni into inch lengths and boil in salted water until tender. Drain and mix in a little granola. Add the sour cream or thick sour milk and about one cup of egg sauce. (See egg sauce recipe, page 156.) Season to taste and bake.

## MACARONI AND CHEESE (VEGETARIAN STYLE NO. 2)

Macaroni, 2½ cups.
Cottage cheese, 1¼ cups.
Milk.
Butter, 1 tablespoonful.
Bread crumbs.

Break the macaroni and cook in salted water until about half done. Drain and pour over it enough milk to cover, and simmer until done. Add the cottage cheese and butter and mix thoroughly. Pour into baking-pan, sprinkle with bread crumbs, and bake.

## MACARONI WITH GRANOLA

Macaroni, raw, 2 cups.
Granola, ½ cup.
Salt to taste.
Cream sauce, 2½ cups.
Butter, 1 tablespoonful.

Cook the macaroni till tender; drain, put one-half in a baking-pan, sprinkle on one-half of the granola, and cover with one-half of the gravy. Repeat with the remainder, making two layers. Bake until nicely browned.

## MACARONI CROQUETTES

Macaroni, raw, 2 cups.
Butter, 1 tablespoonful.
Egg yolks, 2.
Milk, 1 cup.
Flour, 2 tablespoonfuls.
Salt to taste.

Boil the macaroni in salted water until tender, drain, and chop fine. Heat the milk; when boiling, add the butter and flour, that have been rubbed together until smooth; stir until thick, remove from the range, and stir in quickly the beaten yolks of the eggs. Mix this sauce with the macaroni, season with salt, turn out into a flat pan, and let cool. When cold, form into croquettes, egg, crumb, and bake.

## MACARONI NEAPOLITAINE

Vegetable stock, 3 cups.

Diced protose, ½ pound.
Macaroni, raw, 1 cup.
Salt to taste.

Cook the macaroni, drain, and add the rest of the ingredients. Let simmer thirty minutes. Serve.

## MACARONI (SPANISH STYLE)

Macaroni, 2 cups.
Onion, 1.
Cream sauce, 2 cups.
Salt to taste.
Eggs, 3.
Parsley, chopped fine, 1 teaspoonful.
Dash of nutmeg.

Cook the macaroni in salted water, drain, and chop fine; have the eggs boiled hard and chopped fine, and the onions grated. Mix all together, sprinkle with toasted bread crumbs, and brown in the oven. Serve with tomato or Chili sauce.

## MACARONI WITH TOMATO

Stewed tomatoes, 2 cups.
Butter, 2 tablespoonfuls.
Hard-boiled eggs, grated or rubbed through a colander, 1 cup.
Salt.
Vegetable stock, 2 cups.
Macaroni, 2 cups.

Boil the macaroni till tender, drain, and add the stock and tomatoes not strained (they should be put on a sieve and allowed to drain, as the stock will afford sufficient liquid), but chopped, and there should not be enough of them to allow the tomato taste to predominate. Now add to this the hard-boiled eggs, grated or rubbed through a colander. Mix all together, and add a little salt. Pour into a baking-pan about four inches deep, and bake until the mixture is thick. A few lumps of butter sprinkled over the top as it goes to the oven is an improvement.

## SCALLOPED MACARONI WITH VEGETABLE OYSTERS

Vegetable oysters, peeled and sliced, 2 cups.
Macaroni, 1 cup.
Rich milk, 2 cups.
Butter, 1 tablespoonful.
Salt.
Eggs, 2.
Flour, 2 tablespoonfuls.
Bread crumbs.

Boil the macaroni and vegetable oysters separately, and drain. Then place same in alternate layers in a pan. Pour over this a gravy made of the milk, flour, eggs, butter, and salt. Stir carefully so as to get the gravy mixed through thoroughly. Sprinkle a few bread crumbs on top and bake in a quick oven till nicely browned.

## SPAGHETTI IN TOMATO SAUCE

Broken spaghetti, 2 cups.
Flour, 2 tablespoonfuls.
Bay leaves, 2.
Onion, minced, 1.
Tomatoes, 4 cups.

Break the spaghetti into small pieces and boil until well done. Pour over this tomato sauce, made as follows: Brown the minced onion in a little oil, stir in the flour, and add tomatoes, bay leaves, and salt to taste. Let boil, and strain.

## PROTOSE HASH

Protose, 1½ cups.
Cold boiled or baked potatoes, 2 cups.

Oil.
Chopped onions, large, 2.
Salt.
Sage.

Put all together in a pan, pour over a little cooking oil, and set on the stove. When it begins to brown, stir up with a thin knife occasionally until well browned.

## VEGETARIAN HAMBURGER STEAK

Protose, 1 pound.
Sage, ½ teaspoonful.
Eggs, 2.
Nuttolene, ½ pound.
Grated onion, 1 tablespoonful.
Granose biscuits, powdered fine, 2.

Mix thoroughly, form into patties, and fry. Serve with tomato sauce.

## VEGETARIAN HAMBURGER STEAK WITH MACARONI

Serve vegetarian hamburger steak with macaroni and a little brown sauce.

## VEGETARIAN SAUSAGE

Boiled rice, 3 cups.
Grated onion, 6 teaspoonfuls.
Protose, 1 pound.
Salt, 1½ teaspoonfuls.
Oil, 3 tablespoonfuls.
Sage, 6 teaspoonfuls.
Egg, 1.

Form into patties, and roll in gluten or browned flour, and bake in a frying-pan. If browned in the oven, put a small piece of butter on top of each.

## BAKED STUFFED TOMATOES

Tomatoes, medium sized, 6.
Chopped protose, ½ pound.
Sage, ½ teaspoonful.
Chopped parsley.
Toasted bread crumbs, 8 to 12 tablespoonfuls.
Chopped onion, 1 tablespoonful.
Salt, 1 teaspoonful.

Take out the inside of the tomatoes and mix with this the bread crumbs. Then add the other ingredients, and fill the tomatoes, piling mixture up on top. Place small piece of butter on each, and bake in a hot oven, until the tomatoes are cooked. When nearly done, sprinkle chopped parsley over the top.

# *VEGETABLES*

## VEGETABLES

The term "vegetable," as here used, is applied to such plants (grains, nuts, and fruits excepted) as are cultivated and used for food. The use of a large variety of vegetables in our food assists in promoting good health. To get the best results, they should be judiciously combined with nuts, fruits, and grains. Green vegetables are rich in potash salts and other minerals necessary to the system, and in such a form as to be easily assimilated.

Starchy vegetables, as potatoes, supply energy and heat, and give necessary bulk to the food. Peas, beans, and lentils contain a large amount of proteid, used in building and repairing tissue, and are therefore used in place of meat. For weak stomachs they are more easily digested in the form of purees and soups, with the outer indigestible covering removed. All vegetables should be fresh; for in spite of all that may be said to the contrary, all vegetables, whether roots, leaves, or any other kind, begin to lose bulk and flavor as soon, as removed from the ground. The kind that suffer least in this respect are beets, potatoes, carrots, etc. Those which are most easily affected are cabbage, lettuce, celery, asparagus, etc.

Vegetables that have been touched with the frost should be kept in a perfectly dark place for some days. The frost is then drawn out slowly, and the vegetables are not so liable to rot.

# GENERAL DIRECTIONS FOR VEGETABLES

Fresh green vegetables should be cooked as soon after being gathered as possible. Those containing sugar, as corn and peas, lose some of their sweetness by standing. Wash thoroughly in cold water, but unless wilted do not soak. It is better not to prepare fresh green vegetables until they are needed; but if they must be prepared some time before cooking, cover with cold water.

Most vegetables should be put into fresh, rapidly-boiling water, and if cooked in uncovered vessels, they will retain a better color, as high heat destroys their color. In no instance permit them to steep in the warm water, as this toughens them, and in some instances destroys both color and flavor.

The salt hardens the water, and also sets the color in the vegetable. For peas and beans do not add salt to the water until they are nearly done, as they do not boil tender so readily in hard water.

Corn should not be boiled in salt water, as the salt hardens the outer covering of skin and makes it tough. Cook the vegetables rapidly till perfectly tender, but no longer. If vegetables are cooked too long, flavor, color, and appearance are all impaired. To judge when done, watch carefully, and test by piercing with a fork. The time required to cook a vegetable varies with its age and freshness; therefore, the time tables given for cooking serve only as approximate guides.

Delicate vegetables, as green peas, shelled beans, celery, etc., should be cooked in as little water as possible, toward the last the water being allowed to boil away till there is just enough left to moisten. In this manner all the desirable soluble matter that may have been drawn out in cooking is saved.

Strongly flavored vegetables, as cabbage, onions, etc., should be cooked in a generous quantity of water, and the water in which onions are cooked may be changed one or more times.

The general rule for seasoning vegetables is as follows:—

To two cups small whole vegetables, or two cups of vegetables mashed or sliced, add a rounding teaspoonful of butter, and half a level teaspoonful of salt. To beans, peas, and squash, add one-half teaspoonful of sugar to improve them. Add milk or the vegetable liquid when additional moisture is required.

## POTATOES

Pre-eminent among vegetables stands the potato.

The solid matter of potatoes consists largely of starch, with a small quantity of albumen and mineral salts. Potatoes also contain an acid juice, the greater portion of which lies near the skin. This bitter principle is set free by heat. While potatoes are being boiled, it passes into the water; in baking it escapes with the steam.

New potatoes may be compared to unripe fruit, as the starch grains are not fully matured. Potatoes are at their best in the fall, and they keep well during the winter. In the spring, when germination commences, the starch changes to dextrin or gum, rendering the potato more waxy when cooked, and the sugar then formed makes them sweeter. When the potatoes are frozen, the same change takes place.

In the spring, when potatoes are shriveled and gummy, soaking improves them, as the water thus absorbed dissolves the gum, and makes them less sticky. At other times, long soaking is undesirable.

Soak about half an hour in the fall, one to three hours in winter and spring. Never serve potatoes, whether boiled or baked, in a closely covered dish, as they thus become sodden and clammy; but cover with a folded napkin, and allow the moisture to escape. They require about forty-five minutes to one hour to bake, if of a good size, and should be served promptly when done.

## BAKED POTATOES

Potatoes are either baked in their jackets or peeled; in either case they should not be exposed to a fierce heat, inasmuch as thereby a great deal of the vegetable is scorched and rendered uneatable. They should be frequently turned while being baked, and kept from touching one another in the oven or dish. When they are pared, they should be baked in a dish, and oil of some kind added, to prevent their outsides from becoming burned.

## MASHED POTATOES

Pare and boil or steam six or eight large potatoes. If boiled, drain when tender, and let set in the kettle for a few minutes, keeping them covered, shaking the kettle occasionally to prevent scorching. Mash with a wire potato masher, or, if convenient, press through a colander; add salt, a lump of butter, and sufficient hot milk to moisten thoroughly. Whip with the batter whip, or wooden spoon, until light and fluffy. Heap up on a plate, press a lump of butter into the top, and send to the table hot.

## POTATO PUFFS

Potatoes, prepared as for mashed potatoes, 2 cups.
Cream or milk, ¾ cup.
Melted butter, 2 tablespoonfuls.
Eggs, yolks and whites beaten separately, 2.
Salt.

Mix and beat up thoroughly, folding in the beaten whites last. Make into balls, put into greased pans, brush with beaten egg, and bake a light brown.

## MINCED POTATOES

Mince six large, cold potatoes. Put them in a baking-pan, cover with milk; add a little cream, and bake fifteen minutes.

## SCALLOPED POTATOES NO. 1

Potatoes, medium size, 6.
Milk sufficient to cover, mixed with tablespoonful of flour.
Crumbs.
Butter.

Salt.

Cut potatoes into even slices, put in a baking-pan, sprinkle with a little salt, and a few small pieces of butter. Pour over the milk and flour mixture, and sprinkle the top with a layer of crumbs. Cover and bake till potatoes are tender. Remove the cover and brown lightly.

## SCALLOPED POTATOES NO. 2

Cold, boiled potatoes, sliced.
Thin cream sauce.

Place in alternate layers in a pan and sprinkle the top with ground bread crumbs. Bake until brown.

## HASHED BROWNED POTATOES

Use cold, boiled potatoes or good left-over baked potatoes. Pare and cut into three-quarter-inch dice or irregular pieces. Put in a shallow baking-pan, sprinkle with salt, pour over sufficient cooking oil, season well, and prevent scorching. Put into the oven, and when they begin to brown, stir continually till all are nicely browned.

## NEW POTATOES AND CREAM

New potatoes.
Cream.
Salt.
Butter.
Parsley.

Wash and rub new potatoes with a coarse cloth or scrubbing brush; drop into boiling water and boil briskly till done, but no more. Press the potato against the side of the kettle with a fork; if done, it will yield to gentle pressure. In a saucepan have ready some butter and cream, hot but not boiling, a little green parsley, and salt. Drain the potatoes, add the mixture, put over hot water a minute or two, and serve.

## POTATOES A LA CREME

Cold, boiled potatoes, 2 cups.
Parsley, finely chopped.
Flour.
Milk.
Butter, 1 tablespoonful.
Salt.

Heat the milk and stir in the butter cut up in the flour. Stir until smooth and thick. Salt and add the potatoes, sliced, and a very little finely-chopped parsley. Shake over the fire until the potatoes are heated through. Pour into a deep dish and serve.

## POTATOES A LA DELMONICO

Cut the potatoes with a vegetable cutter into small balls about the size of marbles. Put them into stew-pan with plenty of butter and a good sprinkling of salt. Keep the saucepan covered and shake occasionally until they are quite done, which will be in about an hour.

## POTATO CROQUETTES (DELMONICO'S)

Cold, mashed potatoes, 2 cups.
Flour or cracker crumbs.
Salt.
Eggs, 2.
Butter.
Cooking oil.

Season the potatoes with salt and butter. Beat the whites of the eggs and work all together thoroughly. Make into small balls slightly flattened. Dip them into beaten yolks of eggs, roll in flour or cracker crumbs, and fry in hot oil.

## STEWED SALSIFY OR VEGETABLE OYSTERS

Salsify, cut in ¼-inch slices, 1 quart.
Milk, 2 cups.
Butter, 1 tablespoonful.
Salt to taste.

Wash and scrape the salsify, slice, and put into cold water to prevent discoloring. Cook in sufficient boiling water to cover. When tender, drain, add the milk and butter, let simmer a few minutes, and serve.

## ESCALLOPED VEGETABLE OYSTER

Sliced vegetable oyster, 3 cups.
Rich cream sauce.
Sifted bread crumbs.
Salt.

Wash, scrape, cut in thin slices, and put into plenty of cold water till ready to use, to prevent discoloration. When ready to cook, boil in enough water to prevent scorching. Salt when they begin to get tender. Boil a few minutes longer, but do not let them get too salty. Drain, or remove with a skimmer, putting a layer in a baking-pan, then a little rich cream sauce, then another layer of each. Sprinkle the top with sifted bread crumbs, and bake a light brown.

## MOCK OYSTERS

Corn, young and tender, 6 ears.
Flour, 3 tablespoonfuls.
Butter, 3 tablespoonfuls.
Eggs, 3.
Oil.

Salt, 3 teaspoonfuls.

Grate the corn with a coarse grater into a deep dish; beat the whites and yolks separately, and add the corn, flour, butter, and salt. Drop spoonfuls of this batter into a frying-pan with hot oil, and fry a light brown on both sides. The corn must be young.

## CELERY

Cut off all the roots and remove all the decayed and outside leaves. Wash thoroughly, being careful to remove all specks and blemishes. If the stalks are large, divide them lengthwise into two or three pieces and place root downward in a celery glass, which should be nearly filled with cold water.

## STEWED CELERY

Celery hearts, 6.
White sauce, 2 cups.

Cut the celery into half-inch lengths and cook in boiling, salted water. When tender, drain and pour over this the sauce. Heat well, and serve. The liquid drained from the celery may be thickened, seasoned with a little butter, and used instead of the white sauce if preferred.

## LENTILS (ORIENTAL STYLE)

Lentils, 1 cup.
Olive oil, 2 tablespoonfuls.
Salt, 1 level teaspoonful.
Boiled rice, 1 cup.
Onion, finely shredded, 1.

Wash the lentils well, soak overnight, and drain. Cook in boiling water till tender; drain again. Put the olive oil in a saucepan, add the onion, and cook till the onion is soft, not brown. Add the lentils and boiled rice, mix, stir over the fire till hot, add the salt, and serve hot.

www.ingramcontent.com/pod-product-compliance
Lightning Source LLC
Chambersburg PA
CBHW081121080526
44587CB00021B/3697